Lead with AI

How Executives Like You Can Own the Next Decade

Robert Moutal

Medialusion Books

Disclaimer: The field of artificial intelligence is rapidly evolving, and the information, techniques, and best practices discussed in this work reflect the state of knowledge at the time of publication. Readers should be aware that AI technologies, methodologies, and industry standards may change significantly over time. It is recommended to consult current resources and expert guidance when applying the concepts presented herein.

Table of Contents

CHAPTER 1

Introduction: The Octopus Problem

I used to win Emmys the hard way.

Back in the late two thousands, when I was a production manager and then general manager, and later vice-president at Telemundo and Univision San Diego, I had this thing about doing everything myself. TV commercials, news promos, graphics packages. I produced them solo. I was not great at delegating. I was worse at working in big teams. I had the social skills of a very talented hermit crab.

But I was obsessive about control, and I was good at knowing what I liked, even when I could not always explain why. So I just did the work.

Over three or four years, I racked up sixteen Emmys. One night I won five. Another year I was the most nominated person in our entire chapter. I won for animation, art direction, promos, writing, directing, editing, and on-camera performance. The whole menu. I was very proud of that work. I was also completely exhausted, perpetually behind, and slowly becoming the bottleneck in my own career, which is a special kind of irony that only very stubborn people get to experience.

Here is the thing nobody tells you about being a solo operator: you get really good at one thing. You become irreplaceable. And then you hit a ceiling that feels like a wall, and you stand there pressing your face against it wondering why the view is not getting any better. Meanwhile, time passes. The wall does not care.

Then AI happened.

Today, literally today as I am writing this, I translated an entire theatrical play from English to Spanish. Not with a professional translator. Not by outsourcing it to a freelancer who would have charged me two hundred dollars and taken four days. I used an app I built myself called Translato.ai, which I developed entirely by myself, with no computer science degree, no coding background, and no one to blame if something went wrong.

My theater group of twenty-six years had gotten permission from Billy Crystal to stage his play, and the production team needed the script in Spanish. My director, Pepe, sent me the English version in the morning. I sent him the full Spanish translation two hours later.

His response: "What took you so long?"

That was not a complaint. That was a joke. A joke that would have been physically impossible to make five years ago, because five years ago translating an entire theatrical script in two hours was not something one person could do alone, let alone someone who also had three other things on his plate that same morning.

On that same day, I also finished formatting an entire book manuscript. Wrote another book. And built a full presentation deck with presenter notes for a new section of my AI Implementation Lab. I became, functionally, an octopus. Not literally. I still have the standard human number of arms, which is a relief for everyone at the dinner table. But I had developed the capacity to do the work of six people without hiring six people, without burning out harder, and without the chronic low-grade panic that had been my previous productivity strategy.

The quality stayed high. Actually, it got better. Because I am good at knowing what I like. I just was never good at explaining it to other people. AI does not need me to explain it in words. I can show it, push it, redirect it, and refine it until what comes out matches what was in my head. That turns out to be a superpower I did not know I needed because I did not know it was possible.

> *AI does not need you to explain what you want in words. It needs you to know what you want. That is a very different skill, and one you already have.*

This book is about that shift. Not the tools. Not the apps. Not the seventeen-step implementation checklist that someone is definitely selling as a course somewhere. This book is about how leaders who learn to think with AI will operate at a level that leaders who do not simply cannot match, and why the gap between those two groups is opening right now, faster than most people in corner offices want to believe.

Everything in here comes from practice. I built AI-powered software. I run an AI lab where I teach executives and entrepreneurs how to use this technology in their real work, on real problems, this week. I am not a researcher, a futurist, or someone who has spent three years writing a book about something they have never actually done.

I am a practitioner who figured some things out and wants to tell you about them before you waste another year watching from the sidelines.

Let's go.

Part One: The Inflection Point

> *Why this moment is different from every other technology shift (and why that explanation is not just something people say to sell books)*

CHAPTER 2

This Isn't Another Tech Wave (No, Really This Time)

Let me tell you what AI is not.

It is not the internet. It is not the smartphone. It is not the cloud, blockchain, big data, machine learning dashboards, the metaverse, NFTs, or any of the other things someone in a very expensive suit assured you would change everything and then mostly just changed the names of job titles and the length of conference agendas.

Those were waves. You could ride them or miss them and still run a perfectly successful organization. Plenty of companies ignored the internet until 2005 and figured it out just fine. Plenty of executives never learned to code, never understood how the cloud worked, never looked up what blockchain actually was, and went on to have distinguished careers. They hired people who understood the tools. They stayed focused on strategy and leadership. It worked. Good for them.

I want to be careful here, because the temptation when writing a book about AI is to open with a scary statistic. Something like: "By 2028, AI will replace 47 percent of all white-collar jobs." Those statements make for great book marketing. They also cause the kind of low-grade executive anxiety that leads to expensive consulting engagements and very little actual change.

So instead of a scary statistic, I am going to make a specific and defensible claim: AI is not the same kind of shift as previous technology waves. Every previous wave changed what you could do. This one changes what you can think through. And thinking is the thing executives are actually paid for.

Everything else you do, your team could probably also do. Your thinking, shaped by your specific experience, your judgment, your ability to see patterns and make calls under uncertainty, that is what the title and the salary are really about. AI is a direct multiplier on exactly that thing. That is not a productivity story. That is a different story entirely.

A Taxonomy of How Leaders Are Handling This (Spoiler: Most Are Not)

If you spend time in executive circles talking about AI, you start to notice that leaders are sorting themselves into three groups. This is not a formal research finding. It is just what you see when you pay attention to who is in the room and what they actually say versus what they claim to believe.

I call these three groups the Resisters, the Adopters, and the Thinkers. Together, they form what I think of as the RAT Trap, and most leaders are stuck in it without knowing it.

> THE RAT TRAP — Resisters wait for AI to prove itself. Adopters download apps. Thinkers change how they think. The first two groups are the trap. Only one escapes it.

The Resisters: Waiting for a Permission Slip from History

Resisters are waiting for AI to prove itself. They have a list of objections, and they will share those objections with you at considerable length if you let them. Privacy concerns. Data security. Regulatory uncertainty. The sense that someone in an official capacity should probably slow this whole thing down before something unfortunate happens.

None of those concerns are wrong. They are all real issues that thoughtful people are working on. But the conclusion Resisters draw from these concerns, which is that the correct response is to wait and see, is a strategy that is aging very poorly in real time.

Resisters tend to be experienced leaders who got where they are by being rigorous and careful. Those are good qualities in normal times. The problem is that rigor and caution are backward-looking virtues. They protect you from repeating past mistakes. They are considerably less useful when the landscape itself is changing and the past mistakes are no longer the ones worth worrying about.

The Adopters: In the Lobby, Mistaking It for the Building

Adopters are downloading apps. They have ChatGPT on their phone. They asked it to write a performance review once and thought it was pretty good. They use it the way they use spell check: useful, mildly impressive, not something they think about very much.

They will tell you they are exploring AI. Technically, this is not a lie. They have explored the lobby. They have not been upstairs.

The Adopters are the largest group, and they represent both the biggest opportunity and the most common failure mode. They have crossed the threshold of being willing to engage with the technology. But they have not made the mindset shift that turns that willingness into genuine capability. They are collecting tools without developing fluency.

The difference between a tool user and a fluent practitioner is the difference between someone who can order food in French from a menu and someone who can actually have a conversation in French. Both people can get fed. Only one of them can negotiate, improvise, understand what is happening when things go off script, and realize when the waiter is being rude.

The Thinkers: The Dangerous Ones

The Thinkers are the interesting ones. These are the leaders who stopped asking what AI can do for them and started asking how AI changes the way they approach problems. They are not more technical than the other two groups. Most of them could not explain a large language model if you handed them a whiteboard, two hours, and a very patient audience.

But they have developed a working fluency with AI that compounds over time, the way any fluency compounds. Every week they are faster and sharper. They are stress-testing strategy before it reaches the board. They are compressing the competitive intelligence cycle from weeks to hours. They are producing communication at a pace their peers cannot match. And because they are doing this consistently, the gap between them and everyone else is not holding steady. It is widening.

You already know which group you want to be in. That is why you are reading this book. The question is what it takes to get there, and the answer is not more apps.

Why This Particular Wave Is Actually Different, I Promise

Every few years, a technology does something that makes people say this time it is different. And most of the time, it is not. The new technology gets absorbed, integrated, and eventually becomes invisible infrastructure that nobody thinks about, like electricity or Wi-Fi or the guy who figures out how to connect the projector at the beginning of every meeting.

I want to be honest about the fact that claiming this time it really is different carries a burden of proof. So let me be specific.

The reason previous waves did not fundamentally alter executive leadership is that they were about execution, not cognition. The internet made information faster to distribute.

Mobile made it accessible anywhere. Cloud made it cheaper to process. All useful. None of them changed what thinking looked like at the top.

AI changes what thinking looks like at the top. It changes three things that are core to what executives actually do:

First, the speed and depth of analysis. A leader who can run a competitive scenario in forty-five minutes is operating in a different strategic mode than one who has to commission a project and wait three weeks for the deck, by which point the situation has already moved on without them.

Second, the quality of communication. A leader who can draft, pressure-test, and refine a major strategic memo in an afternoon is able to do work that previously required a full communications team and a generous timeline.

Third, the surface area of attention. A leader working fluently with AI can monitor, synthesize, and respond to more information across more domains than was ever possible for a single human. That changes the math on delegation, organization design, and where to spend your personal cognitive budget.

These are not incremental improvements. They are category changes. And they compound in ways that are genuinely hard to appreciate until you are on the far side of them and looking back.

The Window That Is Closing While You Read This

AI fluency is on its way to becoming table stakes for senior leadership. Not a differentiator. Not a nice-to-have. Table stakes. The question is not whether that happens. The question is whether you want to be ahead of it, in it, or cleaning it up afterward.

Based on what I see in my work with executives and in the broader market, we are somewhere between twelve and twenty-four months from AI fluency being a standard expectation in most leadership evaluations, board conversations, and executive hiring processes. The window is closing. Not dramatically. Just steadily, the way all important windows close, which is to say quietly and without announcing itself.

The leaders who make the shift during this window will set the standard. The ones who make it after will meet the standard. Both groups will be fine. But they will not be in the same position. And in some careers, that distinction is the whole game.

The rest of this book is about how to get to the other side of the window while it is still open.

CHAPTER 3

What AI Actually Is (And What It Absolutely Is Not, Stop Saying That)

Before we go any further, we need to get honest about what AI actually is. Not the hype version. Not the dystopian-robots-taking-over version. Not the breathless LinkedIn version where someone discovered that AI could write a subject line and immediately declared the end of the creative industry.

The reason this matters is that most executives are currently thinking about AI in one of two ways, and both of them are wrong in ways that will cause you to make bad decisions.

The too-small framing: it is a fancy autocomplete. A slightly better search engine. A useful tool for junior staff to draft first versions of things so senior people do not have to start from scratch. Helpful. Tactical. Not really a leadership concern.

The too-large framing: it is a superintelligent oracle that will either revolutionize your industry or replace your entire workforce by Thursday, depending on which newsletter you read this morning.

The too-small framing causes you to underinvest in developing real fluency, because you have mentally filed AI under productivity tools for junior people and gone back to your actual work. The too-large framing causes you to either hand the whole subject to IT and stop thinking about it, or to become so preoccupied with the existential implications that you cannot focus on the practical ones.

What you need instead is a working mental model. Accurate enough to be useful. Simple enough to actually remember. Here it is:

> *AI is a system that has processed enough examples of human thinking to be able to participate usefully in human thinking. That is it. That is the whole thing.*

It is not intelligent in the way you are intelligent. It does not have goals, ambitions, feelings, or a secret plan to make your job obsolete. What it does is recognize patterns in language and ideas at a scale and speed that no human can match, and use those patterns to generate responses that are frequently useful, often excellent, and occasionally wrong in ways that are worth knowing about.

The value comes from you bringing your judgment, your context, and your specific problem to a system that can think through it with you faster and with more breadth than any individual human collaborator. It is not replacing your thinking. It is giving your thinking a very capable surface to work against.

What AI Is Genuinely Good At (The Part You Should Underline)

Synthesizing Enormous Amounts of Information Without Complaining About It

If you need to get up to speed on a topic, an industry, a competitor, or a regulatory landscape, AI can compress that research cycle in ways that feel slightly illegal the first time you experience them. This is not just about speed. It is about synthesis quality. A well-constructed AI conversation can turn three hours of reading into a thirty-minute exchange where you come out with a clear map of the landscape, the key debates, the leading players, and the open questions.

For executives who are constantly moving across domains and need to have intelligent conversations about things they are not deep experts in, this is not a minor convenience. It is a material competitive advantage.

Drafting and Refining Communication Without the Blank Page Problem

Most people who try AI for writing give up after the first draft, because the first draft is competent but generic. It sounds like it was written by someone who has read a great deal and felt very little. They conclude that AI cannot write and go back to staring at a blank document, which is also not working, but at least feels like their fault.

The mistake is stopping at the first draft. The real value is in the iteration. You give AI a draft, you tell it what is wrong, it revises, you push back, it adjusts. Three or four rounds produces something dramatically better than round one, and the whole process takes less time than writing a single draft from scratch. Once you have developed your AI drafting rhythm, the quality of your written communication goes up and the time it takes goes down simultaneously. That is not a trade-off you expect to find. It is a genuinely pleasant surprise.

Being the Skeptic in the Room Without Any of the Political Baggage

This is the most underused and highest-value application for senior leaders, and we are going to spend an entire chapter on it. The short version: before you take a major decision to your board, your investors, or your team, you can run it through AI first. Ask it to find every flaw in your reasoning. Ask it to steelman the opposing view. Ask it to play your most challenging board member.

I have had AI change my mind about decisions I felt confident about. Not because the AI was right and I was wrong, but because having to articulate the decision clearly enough to discuss it surfaced assumptions I had not examined. That is the same reason good advisors are valuable. AI does it for free, in private, at eleven at night, without billing you by the hour or telling anyone what you said.

Generating Options You Would Have Filtered Out Before Even Considering

One of the hidden costs of expertise is that it narrows your option set. The deeper your experience in a domain, the more automatically you eliminate approaches that did not work before, that violate conventional wisdom, or that your brain has quietly categorized as not the kind of thing we do here.

AI does not have your experience. It also does not have your filters. Asking it to generate options for a problem you think you have already solved will occasionally produce something that makes you stop and reconsider the framing entirely. This is annoying when it happens and extremely valuable when it does.

What AI Is Not Good At (The Part You Should Also Underline, With a Different Color)

Knowing When It Is Wrong

This is the big one, and I cannot say it clearly enough. AI will state incorrect information with exactly the same confidence as correct information. It does not know what it does not know. It cannot verify its own outputs against external reality. It can produce a beautifully written, completely plausible, entirely wrong analysis and present it to you in the calm, authoritative tone of someone who has never been uncertain about anything.

This does not make AI unusable. It makes AI something you use with your critical faculties fully engaged, not something you outsource your critical faculties to. For every significant output, especially anything involving numbers, facts, or claims that will be repeated to someone else, verify. Not because AI is usually wrong. Because it is occasionally wrong in ways that are not flagged, and the ones that are not flagged are the ones that end up in your board presentation.

Knowing Anything About Your Specific Situation

AI tools are getting better at remembering context across conversations, but they still do not know what you have not told them: the strategic priorities, the team dynamics, the seventeen things that happened last quarter, or why the CFO and the COO are not speaking to each other. The more context you bring in deliberately, the better the output.

Leaders who use AI well have developed the habit of contextualizing their prompts. They do not just ask the question. They provide the situation, the constraints, the relevant history, and what kind of output they need. This habit takes a few weeks to develop and makes an enormous difference in what comes back.

Making the Final Call

This sounds obvious, but it is worth stating because the confidence of AI outputs can create a subtle pressure to defer to them. When AI recommends a course of action in clear, organized, authoritative language, it can feel more credible than it actually is.

The final call belongs to you. AI is one input among several. A useful one, sometimes an excellent one, but one input. Organizations that start treating AI outputs as decisions rather than inputs are not making a technology mistake. They are making a leadership mistake. The technology is just the occasion for it.

The One Mental Model That Changes How You Use All of This

Stop thinking of AI as a search engine that talks. Start thinking of it as a thought partner that never gets tired, never has a bad day, never needs to leave early for a school thing, and has somehow read everything ever written about your industry and seventeen adjacent ones.

A search engine retrieves. A thought partner engages. Those are different activities with different outputs. When you use AI as a search engine, you are asking it to fetch. When you use it as a thought partner, you are asking it to think with you. The second mode is where the disproportionate value for leaders lives, and most people have not made the transition yet.

Practically, this means your prompts will get longer and more specific. You will give more context, ask follow-up questions, push back on responses, ask for alternative framings. It will feel slower at first. It is actually faster at second. And the quality of the output is in a completely different category.

That is the shift. Everything else in this book is built on top of it.

CHAPTER 4

The Authority Cliff (It's Closer Than You Think, and There's No Guardrail)

There is a moment in many executive careers when the ground shifts under you without warning.

It does not look dramatic from the outside. Nobody announces it. There is no memo. But something has changed in the room. The questions directed at you have changed in character. The way people respond when you speak has a slightly different quality. The informal authority you have accumulated over years, the kind that does not appear on any org chart but that everyone in the building can feel, has begun to very quietly erode.

This is the authority cliff. And it is happening to executives right now, in slow motion, in ways that most of them are not fully registering.

The Room Hears Everything You Do Not Say

Here is the dynamic I observe most often: a senior leader, experienced and accomplished, is in a meeting where AI comes up. A use case, a capability, something a competitor is doing. And the senior leader, who has not been actively engaging with AI in their own work, begins speaking in comfortable generalities. Broad statements about potential and risk. The kind of language that sounds authoritative until you listen to it carefully, at which point it sounds like someone who has read the Wikipedia article.

The team hears it. Not the words. The register. The difference between someone who is fluent in a subject and someone who has read about it is audible to anyone who actually lives inside the subject. It is the slight vagueness of the examples. The reliance on received wisdom rather than hard-won observation. The absence of the specific, counterintuitive insight that only comes from doing.

Credibility, once it starts leaking, is very hard to patch. You can give a great speech. You can make a smart call on an unrelated topic. But the specific credibility on the subject that your team has already mentally reclassified you on does not come back easily. It comes back through demonstrated competence over time. That is a longer road than just not losing it in the first place.

> *The authority gap does not open because you stopped being good at your job. It opens because the job is changing, and your team can see it before you can.*

Your Team Already Knows More Than You (and Is Being Very Polite About It)

Here is the part that makes some executives uncomfortable, so I will just say it: in most organizations right now, the people who are furthest along the AI fluency curve are not the most senior people. They are the analysts, the managers, the individual contributors who have been experimenting on their own time because they are interested in it and because they could see immediately how it applied to their work.

They are not talking about it loudly. Organizations that have not explicitly sanctioned AI experimentation tend to create an environment where people are cautious about admitting what they are doing. They have learned, through experience, that bringing new tools to the attention of management is as likely to generate a new approval process as it is to generate enthusiasm.

So they are quietly becoming very good at something that you are supposed to be leading, and they are doing it under the radar, and eventually that dynamic will surface in ways that are more visible and more awkward than a frank conversation about it now would be.

The leaders who get ahead of this do something simple: they ask. They create visible permission for experimentation. They admit, in front of their teams, that they are learning this too. This is not weakness. This is the specific kind of transparency that turns an awkward dynamic into a collaborative one. The leaders who wait for the awkward moment to surface on its own get the awkward moment.

How the Gap Compounds (a.k.a. Why Waiting Is Not Neutral)

The thing about the authority cliff that most people do not account for is that it is not a fixed gap. It is a growing one.

Every month someone spends actively working with AI, they get better at it. They develop instincts about what prompts work. They build a library of approaches that deliver results in their specific domain. They learn faster, work faster, and make better decisions with AI as a tool than they did the month before. This is not dramatic. It is the quiet accumulation of reps.

And every month someone else does not engage, the distance between them and the people who did grows. Not because anything dramatic happened. Just because skill accumulates on one side and not the other.

In competitive sports, this is intuitive. A player who takes a year off does not return to the same level of competition they left. The game moved. Everyone else got better. They come back to a situation where catching up requires more than just resuming where they left off.

Leadership is the same. The leaders who start engaging with AI now are not just further down the same path. In twelve months, they will have developed instincts that cannot be shortcut. You can catch up on knowledge. You cannot catch up on reps.

Four Scenarios That Will Happen to You, in No Particular Order

Let me make this concrete, because abstract arguments about authority and credibility are easy to acknowledge and then ignore.

A board presentation. Your CTO proposes deploying AI in a core business process. You do not have enough fluency to evaluate the proposal on its merits. You can approve it on faith, reject it on instinct, or defer it for more information. None of those feel as good as being able to engage with the substance directly and ask the one question that reveals whether the proposal is well-considered or wishful thinking. Your board notices the difference.

A hiring decision. Two strong finalists. One has clearly integrated AI into their leadership practice in visible, specific ways. The other has not. A year ago, that would not have been a deciding factor. Today it is, at least in organizations that are paying attention. Two years from now, it will be a standard screen for senior roles everywhere.

A talent conversation. One of your best people comes to you with an AI-enabled process improvement they have been developing on their own. If you cannot engage with the specifics intelligently, you have just communicated something about your own limits that you did not intend to communicate. And they noticed. And they are thinking about whether this is the right organization for the next chapter of their career.

A competitor move. Someone in your market does something with AI that changes the competitive dynamic. Your team looks to you for a read. If your read is vague, cautious, and generic, the team forms its own read. The team's read then shapes the organization's response, with or without you.

None of these require you to be a technical expert. They all require you to be fluent enough to lead. That is a lower bar than most leaders think. And the path to it is shorter than the bar implies. What it requires is not genius. It requires engagement.

The Good News, Finally

Here is the part I want you to hold onto as you move into the rest of this book.

You are not starting from zero. The qualities that make someone an effective executive, clear thinking, sound judgment, the ability to ask good questions and recognize good answers, are exactly the qualities that make someone effective with AI. You do not need a different brain. You need the same brain pointed at a new tool.

The learning curve is real but short. In my experience working with executives in my AI Implementation Lab, meaningful fluency develops within weeks of consistent engagement, not months. The first session is disorienting. By the fifth, people are using it to do things they could not have imagined doing alone. By the tenth, they cannot imagine going back.

You are reading this book. That means you are already on the right side of the engagement decision. Everything after this is just practice.

Part Two: The Leadership Mindset Shift

> *How executives need to think differently — before they touch a single tool (this is the part most AI books skip entirely)*

CHAPTER 5

From Knowing to Thinking (What They're Actually Paying You For)

Every organization has at least one executive who has been in the industry for thirty years and has a story for every situation. Ask them about the 2008 financial crisis and they will tell you exactly where they were sitting when Lehman went down, what they did about it, who was in the room, and what kind of sandwich they were eating. The story will be genuinely instructive and will take somewhere between forty-five minutes and the rest of the afternoon.

Their knowledge is real. Their experience is hard-earned. Their instincts are, more often than not, correct. They are genuinely valuable people who have contributed meaningfully to their organizations.

They are also, in many cases, quietly becoming a bottleneck. Not because they forgot anything. Because information itself got cheap.

This is not a new observation. People have been noting since the internet arrived that information is no longer the scarce resource it once was. What has changed with AI is the implication of that observation for senior leadership specifically. If information is cheap, and if the synthesis of information is now also fast and cheap, what exactly are senior leaders being paid for?

The answer is judgment. Which is excellent news, because judgment is the thing that actually takes thirty years to develop. The problem is that most leaders have not updated their operating model to reflect this. They are still running on the assumption that their value comes primarily from what they know, when in fact it comes from how they think.

> *Information was the currency of the old leadership model. Judgment is the currency of the new one. AI just accelerated the exchange rate, whether or not you were watching the market.*

Knowing vs. Thinking: The Distinction That Changes Everything

Let me make this concrete, because it sounds philosophical until you see it play out in an actual decision.

Knowing is holding information. Your industry's typical sales cycle. Your biggest competitor's recent move into the enterprise segment. The return on ad spend of your best acquisition channel. These are things you know. They inform your decisions.

Thinking is what you do with those facts when reality complicates them. When the sales cycle suddenly shortens because a competitor is running a freemium model and your entire go-to-market is built around a long nurture sequence. When the enterprise move might be a brilliant pivot or an overextension and you need to figure out which before your next board meeting. When your best channel starts behaving differently and you need to decide whether it is a trend or noise before you reallocate your budget.

Knowing gives you the inputs. Thinking produces the output. And for most of leadership history, you needed to know a lot to think well, because good thinking required holding enormous amounts of context simultaneously, and the only place to hold context was your head.

AI changes that. AI can hold the context. You bring the judgment. Your head is freed up to do the thing only you can do: apply your specific, experience-shaped, hard-won perspective to a situation that is genuinely novel. That is not a smaller job than the old one. It is a bigger one done better.

Why Knowing You Should Change Is Easier Than Actually Changing

If you have built a career on knowing things, the suggestion that knowing things is less central than it used to be is not exactly welcome news. It is approximately the emotional equivalent of telling someone who has spent thirty years perfecting their handwriting that keyboards exist. Technically helpful. Personally irritating.

The psychological challenge is real and worth naming. Identity is wrapped up in expertise. The way leaders present themselves, the way their authority is perceived, the way they feel confident walking into a difficult conversation, all of that has been historically tied to depth of knowledge. Telling someone that the game has shifted is one thing. Feeling it shift in your gut is something else.

There is also a practical challenge: thinking well with AI requires a skill that most executives have never had to develop explicitly, which is the ability to externalize your own reasoning process.

When you think well in a traditional context, you do it internally. You synthesize information, match patterns against experience, run scenarios, and arrive at a position. You can defend the position if challenged, but you cannot always reconstruct the full path that got you there. That works fine in a world where your judgment is trusted and the decision gets made.

To use AI as a genuine thought partner, you have to externalize that process. Here is the situation. Here are the constraints. Here is what I currently think is going on. Here is what I am uncertain about. Help me think through this. That requires a level of epistemic self-awareness that is a genuine skill. Most leaders have it in conversations with trusted advisors. They just have never been asked to practice it systematically.

The good news is that developing this skill makes you a better leader in ways that have nothing to do with AI. Teams consistently report higher trust in leaders who can articulate their reasoning. It improves decision quality. It makes the organization smarter over time because good thinking is visible and learnable when it is said out loud.

You get the AI benefit and the leadership benefit simultaneously. That is a two-for-one that does not come along very often.

The BRIEF Framework: Writing Prompts That Actually Work

Most of the advice about prompting AI focuses on mechanics. Use this structure. Add this phrase. These tips are not wrong, but they miss the more important point: the quality of a prompt is almost entirely determined by the clarity of your thinking before you start typing.

A bad prompt is a symptom of a fuzzy mental model. You are not sure exactly what you are trying to figure out, so you write something general, get something general back, and conclude that AI is not that useful for your kind of work. This conclusion is wrong but understandable.

A good prompt is a symptom of clear thinking. You know what you are trying to accomplish. You know what you already know and what you are uncertain about. You know what a useful output looks like. When you have that clarity, the prompt almost writes itself.

To develop that clarity consistently, I use a framework called BRIEF. Before opening an AI conversation on anything important, run through these five elements:

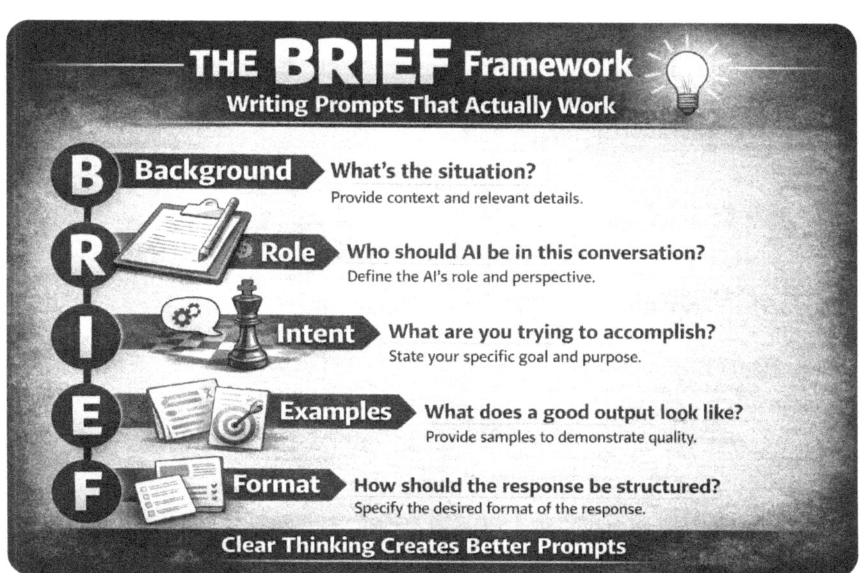

BRIEF — Background: What's the situation? | Role: Who should AI be in this conversation? | Intent: What are you trying to accomplish? | Examples: What does a good output look like? | Format: How should the response be structured?

Background is the context AI needs to engage usefully. Role is often overlooked but enormously powerful: telling AI to be a skeptical board member, a customer advocate, or a hostile competitor produces very different and often more useful responses than a generic request. Intent is your goal, stated as specifically as possible. Examples are the fastest way to communicate quality: show AI what a good version looks like rather than trying to describe it. Format tells AI how to structure its response so you can use it directly.

The whole BRIEF takes three minutes to think through before you start typing. It saves thirty minutes of frustrating back-and-forth on the other side. And it occasionally solves the problem before you even open the AI window, because forcing yourself to articulate all five elements sometimes makes the answer obvious.

That is not a failure of the process. That is the process working exactly as intended.

From Information Hoarding to Judgment Amplification

The old model of executive authority was built on information asymmetry. You knew things other people did not know. You had access to data, context, relationships, and pattern recognition that gave you an advantage in every decision. Protecting that advantage was a rational strategy when information scarcity was a real competitive dynamic.

The new model is built on judgment quality. Information is abundant. Synthesis is cheap. The advantage goes to the person who can take abundant information, apply genuinely good judgment, ask better questions, spot the patterns that matter, and make calls that hold up under pressure.

That is a different skill set from information accumulation. But it is one that AI can amplify in ways it cannot amplify knowledge hoarding. The leaders who make this shift do not become less valuable. They become more valuable, and in a more durable way, because judgment shaped by experience is much harder to replicate or commoditize than an information advantage.

The ones who do not make the shift will find their primary source of authority slowly hollowing out. Not because anyone attacked it. Just because information got cheap and no one told them the model had changed.

Consider yourself told.

CHAPTER 6

Decision Intelligence (Or, the Meeting Where Everyone Agrees with the Boss and Why That's Everyone's Problem)

Let me describe a meeting that has occurred in virtually every organization on earth, probably including yours, possibly including the one you ran last Thursday.

A major decision needs to be made. A room full of intelligent, experienced, well-intentioned people assembles to make it. Someone presents a slide deck. The deck has a recommendation on the last slide. The recommendation is supported by data on the preceding slides. The data was assembled by people who work for the person making the recommendation, which means it was assembled by people with, shall we say, a certain perspective on the outcome.

The meeting then proceeds as follows: the most senior person in the room signals their initial lean. The other people in the room, being rational actors who understand organizational dynamics and enjoy keeping their jobs, update their expressed opinions in the direction of the senior person's lean. The decision that gets made reflects the senior person's initial instinct, polished slightly by the social performance of collaborative process.

Everyone leaves feeling like a decision was made. Technically, one was. Whether it was the right decision is a separate question that will get answered over the following several months, usually in a context that is considerably less pleasant than a conference room.

I am not describing a dysfunctional organization. I am describing how human group decision-making works under conditions of hierarchy, time pressure, and social incentives. It happens in excellent organizations full of excellent people. The excellent people have just never been given a tool for counteracting the dynamic, so the dynamic continues.

AI is that tool. Not because it makes decisions. Because it will push back on yours without any of the career anxiety that makes your team reluctant to do the same.

The Elaborate Theater of How Executives Actually Decide Things

The research on executive decision-making is both fascinating and moderately alarming, depending on how much you enjoy having your self-image intact.

Here is the short version: most executives believe they make decisions through rational analysis. They do not. They make decisions through pattern recognition and intuition, then construct rational justifications afterward. This is not a character flaw. This is how human cognition works under complexity and time pressure. The brain is extremely good at recognizing patterns from past experience and very fast at generating post-hoc explanations for why the pattern match was actually a rigorous analytical process.

The failure mode is specific: this process works well in situations that closely resemble past situations, and fails in situations that are genuinely novel. And the pace at which genuinely novel situations are emerging is, to use a technical term, going up.

So you have leaders making decisions using cognitive machinery optimized for a world that is changing faster than the machinery can update. And a meeting culture designed to produce consensus rather than challenge assumptions. And time pressure that rewards the fast decision over the right one. It is a tremendous amount of structural pressure in exactly the wrong direction.

AI does not fix human psychology. But it gives you a private, patient, socially unconstrained surface for pressure-testing your thinking before it becomes a commitment. That is worth a lot.

> *AI will cheerfully point out every reason your current plan might fail, and do so at eleven o'clock at night, without worrying about what it means for its quarterly review.*

The 4A Pre-Mortem: A Framework for Decisions Worth Getting Right

The pre-mortem is a decision-making technique developed by the psychologist Gary Klein that asks you, before committing to a decision, to imagine that it is twelve months from now and the decision turned out to be a spectacular failure. Not a minor setback. A genuine, expensive, embarrassing disaster. Now work backward: what went wrong?

The pre-mortem is effective because it gives people permission to voice doubts that organizational dynamics would otherwise suppress. In a normal meeting, saying I think this might fail feels like disloyalty or negativity. In a pre-mortem, finding the failure modes is the entire assignment. It changes the social contract of the room.

AI makes the pre-mortem better, and you can run it privately before the decision ever reaches a room. I use a version I call the 4A Pre-Mortem, built around four specific moves:

THE 4A PRE-MORTEM — **Assumptions**: What am I taking for granted that might be wrong? | **Absent Information**: What relevant factors am I not accounting for? | **Adversarial Case**: What is the strongest possible argument against my position? | **Arm's-Length View**: What would I tell someone else to do if this were their decision?

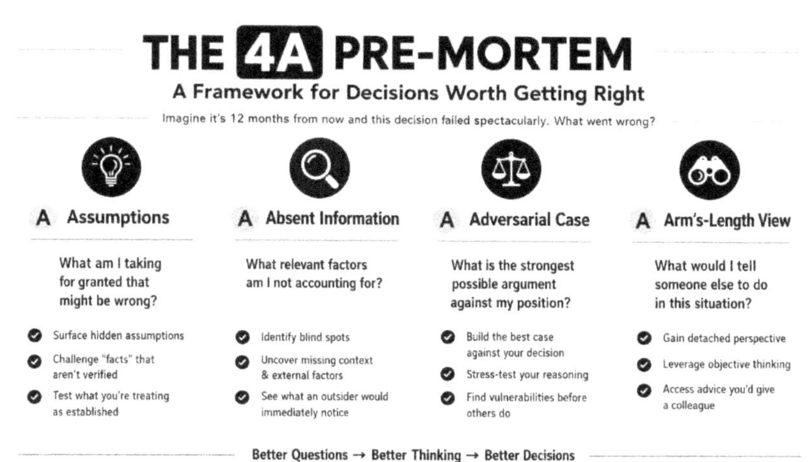

A for Assumptions: What Am I Taking for Granted?

Describe the decision you are leaning toward and ask AI to identify the key assumptions your reasoning depends on. Most of the time, this surfaces two or three things you have been treating as established facts that are actually untested assumptions dressed up in confident language.

I ran this exercise on a pricing decision for one of my products and discovered that my core assumption about what my target customer was willing to pay was not based on research. It was based on my intuition, which felt like research because I had thought about it a lot. These two things are not the same. I found out before launch rather than after. The pricing got adjusted. The launch went better than it would have.

A for Absent Information: What Am I Not Seeing?

Ask AI what relevant considerations your current analysis is missing. Give it the context of your industry, your organization, and the specific decision. Ask what a smart outside observer would notice that you might not.

This works because AI has been trained on an enormous range of business situations and can often surface dynamics from adjacent industries or historical precedents that are relevant to your situation but outside your personal experience. It will not always be right. But it will occasionally say something that stops you, and being stopped on the way to a bad decision is worth a great deal.

A for Adversarial Case: What Does the Best Argument Against Me Say?

Ask AI to construct the strongest possible case against the decision you are leaning toward. Not a weak objection you can dismiss with a wave. The most intelligent, well-evidenced, genuinely uncomfortable argument for the other side.

If you cannot respond to that case clearly after reading it, you are not ready to commit. If you can, you have just significantly strengthened your own position and identified the vulnerabilities you need to address before the decision gets to a room where other people will find them for you.

A for Arm's-Length View: What Would I Tell Someone Else?

Describe your situation to AI as if it were happening to someone else. My colleague runs a company facing the following decision. What would you advise? This technique exploits a well-documented quirk of human psychology: we give better advice to other people than to ourselves because we are less emotionally invested in their outcomes.

By framing your own decision as someone else's, you access a more detached perspective. AI engages with the hypothetical as seriously as it engages with anything else, which means the detachment actually works.

A Practical Note on Speed

I know someone is thinking: this sounds like a lot of process for a decision I need to make by end of day. And that is a fair point.

So let me offer a counterpoint: how much time do you spend cleaning up the consequences of fast decisions that turned out to be wrong? Because that time counts too. It just shows up three months later and has lost its clear causal connection to the original moment when you did not have forty minutes to pressure-test your assumptions.

The full 4A Pre-Mortem takes between thirty and sixty minutes done efficiently. I am not suggesting you run it on every decision. Most decisions do not warrant it. The ones that do, you already know which ones those are. They are the decisions you are still thinking about at eleven o'clock at night. For those ones, an hour of rigorous AI-assisted thinking is not a luxury. It is just due diligence.

CHAPTER 7

The Leverage Equation (Productivity Is a Car. This Is a Plane.)

I want to tell you about two kinds of time savings, because they are not the same thing and almost everyone treats them as if they are.

The first kind gives you more time to do the things you were already doing. You finish your email faster, you prep for meetings more efficiently, you get through your to-do list by four instead of six. This is useful. It is also, in the grand scheme of your career and your organization, roughly equivalent to sharpening your pencils more carefully. Nice. Not transformative.

The second kind changes what you are able to do at all. The things that were previously below the threshold of feasibility, the analysis too expensive to commission, the communication too time-consuming to prioritize, the strategic exploration too slow to compete with the quarterly calendar, those things move above the threshold. What was impossible becomes routine. What was routine becomes instant. The math on what is worth doing changes entirely.

A faster car gets you to the same destination in less time. A plane gets you to destinations that were not practically accessible before. Both are improvements. They are not the same kind of improvement. AI for executives who develop genuine fluency is not a faster car. It is a plane.

I keep coming back to the example from my own life. When I was in television, producing a promo by myself was a multi-day affair. Research, scripting, footage, editing, revisions, approvals. There were things I wanted to make that I never made because the time cost was prohibitive. The idea was good but not good enough to justify a week. The threshold was set by the constraints of human execution.

Now that threshold is somewhere around an afternoon. The math on what is worth doing has changed completely. And the things that became possible as a result, the projects that crossed the threshold, the products I built, the work I shipped, those are not me being more productive doing the same things. They are a fundamentally different relationship with what is possible.

That is leverage. And it is the whole point of this chapter.

> *Productivity means doing the same things faster. Leverage means accessing things that were not possible before. AI offers executives leverage. Most people are still treating it like productivity. The distinction is worth about five years of career trajectory.*

AMP: The Three Places Where AI Leverage Is Disproportionate

Not all of your time is equal. This is obvious when stated directly and routinely ignored in how most executives actually organize their days.

In my work with executives, I have identified three specific domains where AI delivers leverage that is so lopsided it deserves special attention. I call them the AMP framework: Analysis, Messaging, and Positioning. These are not the only areas where AI is useful. They are the areas where the return on developing fluency is so high that if you get good at these three and nothing else, you are already dramatically ahead of where you were.

AMP — Analysis: Compress research, model scenarios, and stress-test strategy at a pace that changes how you prepare for every significant decision. | **Messaging**: Eliminate the blank page, develop your voice, and produce communication that is faster and better simultaneously. | **Positioning**: Build the thought leadership that compounds over time and generates opportunities you cannot yet see.

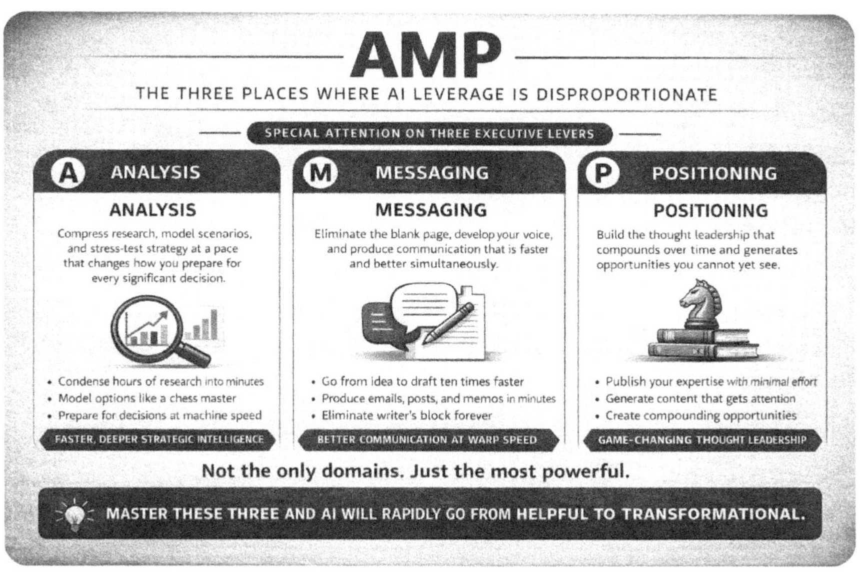

A for Analysis: The Research That Happens Before Breakfast

Every significant leadership decision has an analytical dimension. Market sizing, competitive assessment, risk evaluation, financial modeling. This work is critical. It is also, historically, something that required either significant personal time or a team to do it for you, which meant it happened on a cycle that did not always match the speed of the decisions that needed it.

AI compresses the analytical cycle in ways that feel slightly illegal until you are used to them. I have run competitive analyses in forty-five minutes that would previously have required a research team three days. I have modeled financial scenarios in an afternoon that would previously have required a week of back-and-forth with a CFO and a spreadsheet.

To be precise: I am not saying AI does this analysis better than experienced specialists. In many cases it does not. What I am saying is that AI allows you, as a leader, to do a rigorous first-pass analysis yourself, quickly enough to be genuinely useful for decision-making, without waiting for a formal process to produce a formal output. That changes the tempo of how you lead. It also changes the quality of the conversations you have with your actual analysts, because you arrive already informed and asking specific questions rather than waiting to be oriented.

M for Messaging: Communication That Sounds Like You and Takes a Fraction of the Time

The average senior executive sends somewhere between fifty and two hundred communications a day. Emails, messages, meeting follow-ups, approvals, escalations, recognitions. Each one requires you to translate a thought into language that conveys the right content with the right tone to the right person. This is not trivial. Writing is thinking. Every piece of communication is a small series of judgment calls about what to say, how to say it, and what not to say.

When you are doing that fifty times a day, you are spending a significant fraction of your cognitive budget on execution rather than substance. AI handles the execution. The blank page disappears. The draft arrives. You read it, adjust what is wrong, and send it. Three minutes instead of twenty. Fifty times a day. Do that math across a year and you have recovered something like three hundred hours of executive cognitive capacity.

The key is in the iteration. Nobody sends the first AI draft. You read it, tell it what is off, push it toward your actual voice, and refine until it sounds like you. Over time, as you develop your prompting rhythm, the first drafts require less correction. You are not becoming more like AI. AI is becoming more like you. That is the correct direction.

P for Positioning: The Compounding Asset Most Executives Are Leaving on the Table

Here is an uncomfortable truth about most senior executives: they have more interesting ideas than they ever share publicly. The path from interesting idea to published thought leadership has historically been long, painful, and perpetually displaced by things that feel more urgent, which is to say everything.

I have met executives with thirty years of experience in their field who have never published a single article. They have been meaning to. They have three-year-old drafts somewhere. They know they should. And then another quarter goes by and the body of work that should exist does not, and they feel vaguely guilty, and the cycle continues indefinitely.

AI breaks this specific logjam. Not because it writes for you, but because it eliminates the friction between idea and draft. You talk through what you are thinking, AI shapes it into a structure, you refine it toward your voice, you publish it. Two hours instead of twelve. That is the difference between publishing once a quarter and publishing consistently.

And here is the part worth sitting with: thought leadership compounds. The article you publish today is still out there in six months, eighteen months, three years. Still generating conversations, introductions, and opportunities. The executive who publishes consistently for two years while their peers do not has a visible, searchable, shareable body of work that functions as a permanent asset. The peers have been very busy and have very little to show for it externally.

Positioning is the highest-leverage of the three AMP multipliers for senior leaders, and it is the one most consistently neglected. AI makes it accessible in a way it has never been before. The only remaining obstacle is deciding to do it.

The Two Hundred Hour Argument

Let me put a number on this, because I find that concrete numbers are more persuasive than abstractions, even when the numbers are rough.

If you save four hours per week across the three AMP areas, and that is a genuinely conservative estimate for an executive who has developed real fluency, you have recovered roughly two hundred hours per year. Two hundred hours is five full work weeks.

What would you do with five additional weeks of time that were protected for high-leverage, high-judgment, irreplaceable-you work? What would you start? What relationships would you invest in? What strategic thinking would you actually do instead of planning to do it?

Most executives, when I ask them this question, get a slightly faraway look. Because they know exactly what they would do with that time. They have known for a while. They just stopped believing the time was available.

I am telling you it is available. Not through discipline transformation or calendar restructuring or any of the other things that sound good and do not actually change anything. Through a specific, learnable set of skills that compound over time and are available to you right now.

The leverage equation is in your favor. You just have to decide to do the arithmetic.

Part Three: AI as a Strategic Multiplier

> *Applied frameworks for the domains leaders actually own (not the ones in the org chart, the real ones)*

CHAPTER 8

Strategic Planning with AI (Goodbye, Windowless Conference Rooms)

Every organization I have ever encountered does some version of the following: once a year, the leadership team disappears for two days to a hotel that has the word resort in the name but the ambiance of a mid-century dental waiting room. They sit in a windowless conference room underneath lighting that was apparently designed to discourage optimism, staring at a projected slide that says 2026 Strategic Priorities, and they have a version of the same conversation they had last year, with updated numbers and a new acronym someone found in a Harvard Business Review article during the flight in.

At the end of the two days, they produce a document. The document has a vision statement, some strategic pillars, and a set of goals that are technically measurable but will not be formally measured until next year's retreat, at which point there will be a brief acknowledgment that execution was challenging and a new document with a new vision statement.

I am not describing a dysfunctional organization. I am describing most organizations. The annual strategic planning process is one of the most universally practiced and least rigorously examined rituals in business. It persists not because it works especially well but because everyone does it, it signals seriousness, and nobody has a clearly better alternative to propose.

AI does not fix the annual retreat. The windowless room is on you. But it does fundamentally change what is possible in the strategic thinking that surrounds it, and that turns out to matter considerably more than the retreat itself.

Three Problems with Traditional Strategic Analysis That Everyone Knows About and Nobody Fixes

Traditional strategic analysis has three structural weaknesses that are widely acknowledged and almost never addressed, because the cost of addressing them in a pre-AI world was prohibitive.

The first is speed. A properly executed competitive analysis, market assessment, or scenario planning exercise takes weeks when done by humans. By the time the analysis is complete, the situation it was analyzing has evolved. Decisions get made based on a snapshot of reality from six weeks ago, which in most industries is already something between outdated and misleading.

The second is perspective. The people doing the analysis are inside the organization. They have access to the data, which is good, but they also have the organization's assumptions, blind spots, and internal politics baked into their worldview. The analysis reflects what the organization already believes at least as much as it reflects what is actually true outside the building.

The third is coverage. There is simply too much relevant information for any team to synthesize fully. Competitor moves, regulatory shifts, technology developments, customer behavior changes, macroeconomic signals, adjacent industry dynamics. Every analysis makes choices about what to include and exclude, and those choices are rarely explicit. The most important things are sometimes the ones that fall through the gaps, not because they were judged unimportant, but because nobody was looking in that direction.

AI does not eliminate any of these problems. It attacks all three of them in ways that change the strategic conversation enough to matter.

Scenario Planning in an Afternoon, or: What Were We Doing with All That Time?

Scenario planning is the discipline of developing multiple plausible futures and thinking through the implications of each. It was pioneered by Shell in the 1970s, refined by decades of strategy consultants, and is now taught in every MBA program as a foundational strategic tool. It is also, in practice, almost never done well outside large organizations with dedicated strategy functions, because it is time-consuming, hard to facilitate well, and requires a kind of structured imagination that does not come naturally in organizations built around execution.

With AI, the process becomes feasible for any leader with a few hours and a clear description of their situation.

You describe your organization, your market, and your current strategic position. You identify the two or three most important uncertainties facing your business over the next three years. Not risks you can quantify. Genuinely open questions where the answer significantly changes what the right strategy is. Will the regulatory environment tighten or loosen? Will AI commoditize your core service or enhance it? Will your primary customer segment consolidate or fragment?

You give AI those uncertainties and ask it to develop scenarios: what does the world look like if each uncertainty resolves favorably, and what does it look like if it does not? What would you do differently in each scenario? Which moves are robust across all scenarios? Which are bets on a specific outcome?

What comes back is not a finished strategy. It is a structured thinking surface that gives your actual strategic conversation much better raw material to work with. An hour of that process produces more useful material than most two-day retreats, and you arrive at the retreat already knowing what you think rather than waiting for the group conversation to tell you.

> *The goal of AI-assisted scenario planning is not to predict the future. It is to make sure you have thought seriously about several versions of it before one of them arrives.*

The War Game Your Strategy Team Never Has Time to Run

The war game is a classic strategy tool that most organizations acknowledge is valuable and almost never actually do. You simulate a competitive scenario by having a team fully inhabit your competitor's perspective and think through how they would respond to your moves. The insight comes from genuinely taking the other side rather than imagining the other side while remaining yourself.

The reason war games rarely happen is that they require people to convincingly inhabit a perspective that is not their own, and to do so rigorously enough that the exercise produces genuine surprise rather than confirmation of what everyone assumed the competitor would do. That is hard. People keep slipping back into their own perspective. The team playing the competitor keeps making the decisions they would make, not the decisions the competitor would make.

AI is remarkably good at this. You give it everything you know about your primary competitor: their public statements, strategic moves, leadership philosophy, customer base, pricing structure, stated priorities, known pressures. You tell it you are about to make a specific move and ask what that competitor would do in response.

Then you play it out. We are going to counter with this. What do they do next? You run it through several rounds. The result is not a perfect prediction of competitor behavior. It is a much more rigorous pressure test of your strategy than anything that happens in most boardrooms.

I ran one of these exercises with a client who was planning to enter a new market segment. The war game surfaced a response from the incumbent player that my client had not accounted for. It was plausible enough that they built a contingency plan. Six months later, the incumbent responded almost exactly as the simulation had suggested. The contingency plan was executed. The market entry succeeded. My client attributes this specifically to having thought through the scenario in advance rather than encountering it as a surprise.

I am not claiming AI predicted the future. I am claiming that taking the competitor's perspective seriously, which AI made feasible to do thoroughly, produced better preparation than ignoring it would have.

What AI Gets Wrong About Strategy (the Honest Part)

AI is trained on the past. It has a strong gravitational pull toward conventional wisdom in any domain, because conventional wisdom is what the vast majority of the text it trained on reflects. When you ask it about strategy, you will get responses that pattern-match to established frameworks and accepted best practices. This is useful as a baseline. It is a trap if you are in a situation where conventional wisdom is part of what you are trying to escape.

AI does not know your organization's actual execution capacity. Strategy is always partly what is theoretically correct and partly what this specific team can actually do given their history, dynamics, and capabilities. AI is far better at the first part than the second. The second part is where your judgment is irreplaceable.

AI can be confidently wrong about specific facts. Industry data, competitor details, regulatory specifics. Verify anything that will be repeated to someone else.

With those caveats in plain sight: AI-assisted strategic planning is still dramatically better than the alternative for most organizations. The alternative being two days in a room with no windows and sandwiches that arrive at eleven-thirty.

CHAPTER 9

Communication at Executive Scale (Your Voice, Amplified, Finally)

Abraham Lincoln, according to a story that is possibly apocryphal but deeply satisfying, once received a complaint that Ulysses Grant drank too much whiskey. Lincoln's alleged response was to ask what brand Grant was drinking and send a case to his other generals. The point being: results matter more than methods, and the methods of successful people are worth studying even when they are unconventional.

I think about this story when I encounter executives who are uncomfortable about using AI to help with their communication. There is a lingering sense in some circles that using AI to draft or refine your writing is somehow inauthentic. That the words should emerge fully formed from your own skull, or they are not really yours.

This position is both understandable and historically uninformed. Every major American president has had speechwriters. Every significant CEO has a communications team. Every published author has an editor who occasionally makes the writing better than the writer would have made it alone. The idea that executive communication should be unassisted is a romantic notion with very little connection to how high-stakes communication has worked throughout history.

Collaboration is not inauthenticity. The question is not whether you are getting help. The question is whether the ideas are yours and whether you genuinely endorse what gets published under your name.

With AI, the ideas are yours. The structure, the drafts, the iteration, those are collaborative. Your judgment, your perspective, your hard-won point of view, the thing that makes your communication worth reading, that is entirely yours. AI just means you do not have to spend four hours staring at a blank page before any of it gets out.

> *The blank page is not where great thinking lives. It is where great thinking goes to die of boredom and mild embarrassment. AI removes the blank page. What you put on it remains entirely yours.*

The Executive Voice Problem (Everyone Has One, Nobody Talks About It)

Most executives have a voice. A way of framing things, a set of recurring ideas, a perspective that people who know them would recognize in a sentence. In conversation, that voice comes out naturally. They are relaxed, specific, occasionally funny, sometimes blunt, always recognizable as themselves.

In formal writing, it frequently disappears. Replaced by something that sounds like a committee wrote it while trying to avoid saying anything quotable. The vocabulary becomes formal. The sentences become passive. The point becomes hedged. The whole thing reads like a person pretending to be an organization.

This is not a character flaw. It is what happens when writing feels high-stakes. The informal, specific, recognizable you gets buried under the weight of wanting to get it right. And the result is communication that is technically correct, professionally appropriate, and almost completely forgettable.

AI helps with this in a way that feels counterintuitive until you experience it: working with AI to draft and refine your communication forces you to articulate your voice more explicitly than you normally would. When you read an AI draft and say that is not how I would say it, you have to get specific about what you mean. And the process of being specific about what you mean is the process of discovering and defining your own voice.

Over time, as you develop your AI drafting workflow, the first drafts require less correction because AI has learned your patterns. You are not becoming more like AI. AI is becoming more like you. The direction matters. Most people get this backward.

The Email That Ended a Relationship You Were Pretty Sure Was Fine

The average executive email is written under time pressure, usually between other things, often on a phone while doing something else, and read by the recipient in a completely different context than the one it was written in.

The result is that tone gets misread constantly. The email you wrote in thirty seconds while boarding a plane reads as terse and dismissive to someone who spent three days on the project it is responding to. The email you wrote as a casual check-in reads as a formal expression of concern to someone who is already anxious about their position. The email you thought was clear is interpreted in four different ways by four different people, three of which create problems you did not intend.

AI does not eliminate these problems. Human beings will continue to be human beings, and human beings are remarkably inventive when it comes to misreading each other. But AI gives you a fast way to sanity-check important communication before you send it.

Paste your draft into an AI conversation and ask: how does this read? Does the tone match what I intend? What might the recipient infer that I did not mean to imply? Is there anything in here that could land differently than I expect?

You will not do this for every email. Nobody has time for that, and most emails do not warrant it. You will do it for the ones that matter: the ones going to people who are in a difficult moment, the ones that touch sensitive dynamics, the ones where you know the relationship is important enough that a misread would cost you something real. The time investment is ninety seconds. The return is not having to spend two weeks repairing a relationship that a better-written email would have maintained.

Thought Leadership at Scale, or: Publishing What You Have Been Meaning to Publish Since 2019

Here is an uncomfortable observation about most senior executives: they have more interesting ideas than they ever share publicly. The path from interesting idea to published thought leadership has historically been long, painful, and chronically deprioritized.

I have met executives with decades of genuine expertise in their field who have never published a single article. They have been meaning to. They have drafts that are years old. They know they should be doing it. And then another quarter goes by and the body of work that should exist still does not, and they feel vaguely guilty about it, and the guilt does not actually produce an article, and the cycle continues.

AI breaks this specific logjam. Not because it writes for you. Because it eliminates the friction between idea and draft. The process is simple: talk through what you are thinking, in whatever form it is in. A voice memo. A rough paragraph. A few bullet points. AI takes that raw material and gives you a shaped first draft. You read it, mark what is wrong and what does not sound like you. You revise. Repeat two or three times. Total time from idea to publishable article: two to three hours instead of twelve.

That is the difference between publishing occasionally and publishing consistently. And consistent publishing compounds in ways that occasional publishing does not. The article from eighteen months ago is still out there. Still being read, shared, referenced. Still generating conversations and connections and opportunities that have nothing to do with how much time you have had recently.

The executives who use AI to build their thought leadership over the next two years will have a visible, searchable, shareable body of work that their peers, who are still treating writing as too time-consuming to prioritize, will not have. That asymmetry is already building. It will be very visible in three years.

Speeches, High-Stakes Presentations, and the Difference Between Being Heard and Being Remembered

Every executive has at least one presentation a year that actually matters. Not the routine board update. Not the monthly all-hands where everyone is half-reading email. The keynote at the conference. The investor day. The company-wide speech at a moment of genuine change. The kind of communication where people leave having formed a view about you, one way or another.

The preparation process for this kind of communication has traditionally been either very long or very expensive or both. AI changes that significantly. The process I use and recommend starts not with the content but with the goal.

Before touching a word of the speech itself, ask and answer three questions: What do you want people to feel when they leave the room? What do you want them to do differently as a result? What is the one thing you want them to remember six months from now? Getting clear on those answers before you touch the content is worth more than any amount of time spent polishing language.

Then tell AI your three or four most important points and ask it to help you find the story that carries them. The best speeches are not organized around information. They are organized around narrative. Something happened. Something changed. Something matters now that did not before. AI is good at finding the narrative architecture that makes your specific content land with a specific audience.

Then draft, refine, and read it out loud, because the spoken word and the written word are genuinely different things. What reads well on paper frequently sounds stilted coming out of a human mouth. Ask AI to identify places where the language is too dense, too formal, or too written to actually say in front of an audience. It will find them. Your delivery will be better for it.

The Ghostwriting Question, Answered Directly

You have been wondering about it, so here is the answer without the usual hedging.

The standard I use is what I call the ownership test. If the ideas are yours, the perspective is yours, and you read the final draft and genuinely endorse every sentence in it as something you believe and would say, then it is your communication. The process that produced it is your business. Editors, speechwriters, and communications teams have been helping leaders produce better communication for as long as leaders have existed, and nobody suggests that this makes their ideas less theirs.

If the ideas are not yours, if you are attaching your name to AI-generated content that does not represent your actual views in order to borrow credibility you have not earned, that is a different problem entirely. It is not a technology problem. It is an integrity problem. AI just makes that particular form of dishonesty easier to do, which means it also makes it easier to do poorly.

The test is simple: do you genuinely believe everything in this, and are you willing to defend it in a live conversation? If yes, publish. If no, revise until you can say yes. That is the whole framework.

CHAPTER 10

Talent in the AI Era (Someone on Your Team Is About to Quit, and You're the Last to Know)

At some point in the not-too-distant future, someone on your team is going to hand in their notice. When you ask why they are leaving, they will give you a polished, reasonable answer about career growth and new opportunities and wanting to explore what else is out there. This answer will be technically true and will not include the actual reason, which is that they found an organization that lets them work with AI the way they want to work with AI, and yours does not.

This has already started happening. It is going to accelerate.

The people who are most fluent with AI tend to share certain qualities: they are smart, highly productive, mildly impatient with friction, and acutely aware that their skills are in demand. They are not primarily motivated by money, though they will leave for money if they feel undervalued. They are motivated by the opportunity to do interesting work at a pace that matches their capability.

If your organization is one where AI-fluent people have to work around approval processes, justify every tool they want to use to a risk committee that is still thinking about AI the way it thought about social media in 2011, and watch their AI-enabled productivity get treated as invisible rather than celebrated, those people will eventually leave. Not immediately, usually.

People give organizations more chances than the organizations probably deserve. But the calculus is running continuously, and it tips.

The New Talent Math That Most Org Charts Have Not Caught Up To

AI is changing the relationship between roles and output in ways that organizational structures are not yet reflecting.

Historically, output was roughly proportional to headcount. You needed more output, you added people, you got more output. This was never perfectly true, but it was reliable enough that headcount became a proxy for organizational seriousness. Big team means real company. Small team means scrappy startup.

AI disrupts that proxy. A single person with genuine AI fluency can produce the output of three or four people in many knowledge work roles. This is not universally true. There are roles where the value is relational, physical, or institutional and AI does not touch the core of the job. But in roles that are primarily about producing knowledge, writing, research, analysis, communication, and code, the leverage effect is real and it is significant.

This creates a talent calculus problem most organizations are not yet having explicitly. Do you hire three people with average AI fluency, or one with exceptional AI fluency? Do you pay a premium for AI-fluent candidates in high-leverage roles? Do you invest in developing AI fluency in your existing team?

The organizations that are getting this right are not necessarily the ones paying the most. They are the ones that have decided AI fluency matters and made that decision visible in how they hire, develop, and recognize people.

> *The most dangerous talent assumption in most organizations right now is that AI fluency is a nice-to-have for individual contributors. It is becoming a job requirement. The roles just haven't been updated to say so yet.*

Finding the People Who Are Already Ahead of You

In most organizations, AI fluency is distributed unevenly and the distribution does not follow the org chart. The people who are furthest along the curve are probably sitting somewhere in the middle of your organization, in roles that are not senior enough to have attracted your explicit attention on this topic. They have been experimenting on their own time because they found it interesting and could see immediately how it applied to their work.

They are almost certainly not talking about it loudly. Organizations that have not explicitly endorsed AI experimentation tend to create environments where doing it feels vaguely unauthorized, like using your personal email on the company Wi-Fi. People learn quickly whether new tools are welcomed or tolerated, and tolerated is not enough to produce open sharing.

The way to find them is embarrassingly simple: ask. Explicitly. A message that says something like: we are thinking seriously about how to integrate AI into our work and I want to hear from people who have been experimenting. If you have been using AI tools and have thoughts on how we could do more with this, reach out.

You will hear from people you did not expect. Some of what they tell you will genuinely surprise you. And the act of asking publicly does something beyond finding the people: it signals that this is now a conversation the organization is having, which gives everyone else permission to have it too.

Building an AI Culture Without Forming a Committee About It

Somewhere in a major corporation right now there is a Chief AI Officer, a VP of AI Transformation, an AI Center of Excellence, an AI Steering Committee, and an AI Ethics Working Group, and the sum total of AI-related activity in that organization is five times the meetings and one-fifth the actual experimentation of a company a tenth its size whose CEO just started using AI personally and told the team to try things.

I am being slightly uncharitable. But only slightly.

The organizations making genuine progress on AI adoption are not the ones with the most sophisticated AI governance structures. They are the ones where senior leadership has made it visibly, unambiguously clear that experimentation is expected, failure is acceptable, and people who find useful applications will be recognized for it. That is a culture decision. It costs nothing except the willingness to mean it.

The signals your team is watching for are simpler than most leaders think.

First signal: you use AI yourself, and you say so. When AI changes your view on something in a meeting, mention it. When you ask your team to prepare something and suggest they use AI to accelerate the work, say that explicitly. Leaders who model behavior produce more behavior change than leaders who mandate it. This is true for every cultural shift and it is emphatically true here.

Second signal: you protect space for experimentation. The enemy of AI adoption in organizations is not skepticism. It is the absence of any time not already claimed by something urgent. Even a small protected space, even a few hours a week, where experimentation is the actual assignment rather than the thing you do instead of your assignment, changes the signal the organization is receiving.

Third signal: you celebrate what works. When someone figures out a useful AI application, get them in front of the team to share it. Not a formal presentation with a deck. A ten-minute conversation. Here is what I tried, here is what happened, here is what I would do differently. That kind of knowledge transfer compounds fast in organizations that have the habit of it.

What Happens to the Roles: The Question Nobody Wants to Ask Out Loud

I want to address the question that is in the back of every room when AI and talent come up together, which is: if AI can do a significant fraction of the work currently done by certain roles, what should those roles become?

The wrong answer is: eliminate the roles and capture the savings. I say this not because it is morally wrong, though there are moral dimensions worth engaging with, but because it is strategically shortsighted. Organizations that eliminate roles and do nothing else will briefly look efficient. Then they will hit situations where AI fails, where nuance is required, where the institutional knowledge that lived in those people simply does not exist anymore, and they will find out the hard way what they traded away.

The right answer is harder and more interesting: what can these roles become when the execution burden is lifted? The analyst spending sixty percent of their time pulling and cleaning data can now spend that time on interpretation and strategic recommendation. The communications professional spending half their time drafting routine content can focus on the communication that requires genuine craft and relationship. The HR professional buried in administrative tasks can do the actual human work of developing people.

Every role in your organization has a higher-leverage version of itself waiting to emerge when AI handles the lower-leverage execution. The leaders who help their people find that version will build organizations that are more effective and more attractive to excellent people simultaneously.

The leaders who use AI primarily as a headcount reduction tool will save money in the short run and lose something harder to quantify in the long run. Judgment, relationships, and institutional knowledge live in people. They do not transfer to a software subscription, however good the software is.

CHAPTER 11

Innovation and Competitive Advantage (And Why Sticky Notes Are Not a Strategy)

Innovation has a branding problem.

At some point, the concept got hijacked by an aesthetic. Innovation means a whiteboard covered in color-coded sticky notes. Innovation means a brainstorming session where all ideas are good ideas, which is another way of saying no ideas get evaluated, which is another way of saying nothing useful comes out but everyone feels heard. Innovation means a hackathon where your most technically interested employees spend a weekend building something that will never be deployed, eating cold pizza and feeling temporarily important before returning to their regular jobs on Monday.

I have nothing against sticky notes, pizza, or people feeling temporarily important. I object to the theatrical version of innovation that substitutes process for outcome and enthusiasm for result. Real innovation, the kind that produces sustainable competitive advantage, is less visually exciting and considerably more useful. It is the slow accumulation of small improvements, the willingness to follow an uncomfortable insight to its conclusion, and the organizational discipline to implement something actually different rather than just talk about it.

AI changes the economics of real innovation in ways that matter. Not in a way that will make your next offsite more photogenic. In a way that makes more things worth trying.

The Actual Constraint on Innovation (It Is Not Ideas)

The traditional constraint on innovation in most organizations is not the quality or quantity of ideas. Most organizations have more potentially useful ideas than they have bandwidth to investigate. The ideas that get investigated are the ones with a visible champion, or the ones that come from the right level of the org chart, or the ones that fit neatly into the existing planning and budget cycle. The rest die quietly in someone's notebook or annual review.

The real constraint is the cost of testing ideas. Specifically: the overhead of running even a modest internal project is so high in most organizations that the bar for what gets investigated is set far above where it should be. You need a business case. You need budget approval. You need headcount. You need to convince someone three levels up that the idea is worth their attention before you have done a single hour of work to find out if it actually is.

AI reduces the cost of initial investigation dramatically. The question that previously required a formal research project to answer can now be explored in an afternoon. The competitive landscape that took a team a week to map can now be sketched out in a few hours. The financial model that required a two-day collaboration between finance and strategy can now be drafted in the morning and pressure-tested by lunch.

This does not mean every idea becomes viable. It means the threshold for finding out whether an idea is viable drops substantially. You can run more experiments. You can kill bad ideas faster. You can find the ones worth real investment more efficiently. The net result is a higher quality innovation portfolio and a lower cost to build it.

Spotting Market Shifts Before Your Competitors Do (Without Being Psychic)

Every industry has weak signals. Early indicators that a market is about to move, a customer behavior is about to change, a regulatory environment is about to shift, a technology is about to make something possible that was not possible before. Most organizations pick up on these signals eventually. The question is whether they do so early enough to prepare or late enough that they are reacting.

The organizations that spot shifts early tend not to have better information than their competitors. They process the same information more rigorously. They read the same reports, attend the same conferences, talk to the same customers. The difference is in what happens after the encounter with new information.

The practice I find most useful for this is what I call the So What Chain. When you encounter something that seems potentially significant, you ask AI: so what does this imply? Then you ask: and what does that imply? You run the chain out several levels until you reach either a genuine strategic implication or the point where the speculation has outrun the evidence.

This sounds simple. It is simple. The hard part is doing it consistently. Most executives read something, have a vague sense that it is interesting, and move on to the next thing in their inbox. The information entered their awareness and produced no output. The So What Chain forces an output. It turns a passive encounter with information into an active thinking exercise, and the thinking exercises that happen consistently before a shift becomes obvious are worth far more than the ones that happen after.

> *The leaders who spot market shifts early are not smarter or better-informed than their competitors. They are more disciplined about following an insight to its conclusion before moving on. AI makes that discipline faster and easier to maintain.*

The Small Bets Framework: Running Experiments You Can Actually Afford

I am a committed advocate of the small bets approach to innovation, and AI makes it more viable than it has ever been for organizations that do not have Google or Amazon's budget for failed experiments.

The concept is straightforward: rather than placing a small number of large, expensive, slow bets, you make a large number of small, cheap, fast ones. You expect most to fail. You are looking for the few that work well enough to justify larger investment. The key constraint is that the experiments have to be genuinely small: small enough that failure is not damaging, fast enough that you learn quickly, and numerous enough that you get meaningful signal.

The traditional objection in most organizations is that small bets are not actually small when you account for the organizational overhead. Even a modest internal project requires headcount, budget, management attention, and coordination across teams. The friction of running an experiment often matches the size of the experiment itself, which means you cannot run very many before you have consumed your entire capacity for initiative.

AI changes this overhead calculation significantly. An experiment that can be designed, modeled, and pressure-tested with AI requires much less of the organizational machinery that made traditional experiments expensive. You can sketch the idea, model the unit economics, test the key assumptions, and develop a minimum viable version faster than you could previously have written the project brief.

The practical implication: if your organization is currently able to run four or five meaningful innovation experiments per year, AI should allow you to run twenty or thirty. The ones that fail will fail faster and cheaper. The ones that work will surface sooner. The overall return on your innovation investment goes up, not because you got smarter, but because the cost structure changed.

Curiosity as a Competitive Asset

I want to end this section with something that gets underrepresented in most conversations about organizational AI adoption, which is the role that genuine intellectual curiosity plays in whether any of this actually happens.

Every framework in this chapter, the So What Chain, the small bets approach, the systematic processing of weak signals, requires someone to actually do it. And that someone will not be executing it because it was mandated or included in their annual goals. It will be someone who finds the process genuinely interesting and has enough organizational permission to prioritize it.

Curiosity is not a training initiative. You cannot manufacture it by sending people to workshops. What you can do is build an environment where it is rewarded rather than quietly penalized.

Where someone who spends two hours exploring an idea that turns out to be a dead end is not seen as having wasted two hours. Where the instinct to follow an interesting signal is treated as a feature rather than a distraction from the actual work.

The organizations that build that environment will have teams that are continuously learning, experimenting, and finding the small insights that, over time, accumulate into advantages that are very hard to compete with. The organizations that optimize purely for predictability and immediate output will have teams that do exactly what they are told, efficiently and reliably, right up until the moment when doing exactly what they were told stops being enough.

AI gives your curious people more to be curious with. It lowers the cost of following an instinct to see if it goes anywhere. It makes the exploration of ideas fast enough that it is no longer an unreasonable use of a Monday afternoon.

Build the culture where that is welcomed. The rest takes care of itself.

Part Four: Building Your AI-Ready Organization

> *From personal fluency to organizational capability (without forming a steering committee about it)*

CHAPTER 12

The AI-Ready Culture (Which Is Just a Regular Culture That Stopped Being Afraid)

Culture change has a reputation problem.

Mention it in a meeting and watch what happens to people's faces. The enthusiasm drains. The eyes go slightly unfocused. Someone starts checking their phone. This is because, in most organizational contexts, culture change is code for a multi-year initiative with a consultant, a framework with a catchy name, a series of workshops that produce laminated values statements nobody can remember, and approximately zero measurable difference in how anyone actually behaves on a Tuesday afternoon.

I want to be clear that when I say AI-ready culture, I mean something much simpler and considerably more achievable than that. I do not mean a transformation initiative. I do not mean a change management program. I mean an organization where people feel safe experimenting with AI, where the ones who figure something useful out share it with the rest, and where the senior leadership makes it unambiguously clear by their own behavior that this is a thing we do here now.

That is it. That is the whole culture change. The rest is implementation details.

The Enemy of AI Adoption Is Not Skepticism, It's Tuesday

Most leaders, when they think about why AI adoption is slow in their organizations, assume the problem is resistance. People do not want to change. People are comfortable with the old way. People are skeptical of new technology. These things are sometimes true. They are not usually the main problem.

The main problem is Tuesday. Specifically, the fact that Tuesday is completely full. There is a deliverable due, a meeting that ran long, an email thread that needs resolution, and a report that was due last Thursday. In this environment, experimentation with new tools is not something people resist. It is something they genuinely intend to do and genuinely cannot find the time for. The calendar is the adversary, not the mindset.

The leaders who solve this do not do it by convincing people that AI is important. Their people already know AI is important. They do it by creating the conditions under which experimentation can actually happen. A protected hour. A standing agenda item where people share what they tried. A team meeting where someone is explicitly invited to show the group something they figured out with AI. These are not culture transformation initiatives. They are scheduling decisions.

Schedule a thing, name it, protect it from the inevitable gravitational pull of urgent work, repeat it for six weeks. That is your culture change.

> *Nobody changes their behavior because they were persuaded that change is important. They change because the environment made it possible and then made it normal.*

The Three Signals Your Team Is Watching For

Your team is not waiting for a formal announcement about your AI strategy. They are watching your behavior and drawing their own conclusions about what is actually endorsed here, as opposed to what is officially endorsed.

These are the three signals that matter, in roughly descending order of impact.

Signal One: You Use It Yourself and You Say So

This is the highest-leverage thing a leader can do and the one most consistently skipped. When you use AI to prepare for a meeting, mention it. When an AI analysis changes your view on something, say so in the room. When you ask your team to produce something and you think AI could accelerate the work, suggest it explicitly rather than leaving it as an implied option that nobody is quite sure is sanctioned.

Leaders who model behavior change get more behavior change than leaders who mandate behavior change. This is not a novel insight. It is one of the most reliable findings in organizational behavior. And yet most leaders announce AI initiatives without changing their own visible behavior at all, then wonder why the announcement did not produce the adoption they hoped for.

The announcement is not the signal. You are the signal.

Signal Two: Failure Is Actually Okay

Most employees have a finely calibrated sense of when failure is theoretically acceptable versus when it is actually acceptable. Leadership communications on this topic are not trusted. Behavior around actual failures is trusted completely.

The first time someone on your team experiments with AI in their work, produces something imperfect, and brings it to your attention, your response determines the next six months of AI adoption in your organization. If your response is anything other than genuinely curious and encouraging, the signal that goes through the team is: experimentation with AI is something we say we want and do not actually want. Adjust your behavior accordingly.

The fastest way to build an AI-ready culture is to celebrate a well-intentioned AI experiment that did not work, visibly and explicitly. Share what was learned. Thank the person for trying. Make it clear that this is what we want more of. That one moment is worth more than any amount of cultural programming.

Signal Three: The People Who Figure It Out Get Recognition

This does not have to be formal recognition. Informal recognition is often more powerful. Inviting someone to share what they figured out with a team. Mentioning in a broader conversation that a person developed a useful approach. Asking someone to become the team's go-to resource on a specific AI application.

Recognition signals priority. When people see that AI fluency leads to visibility and opportunity, the adoption curve bends. When they see that it leads to nothing in particular, the adoption curve flattens. People are rational. They invest their discretionary time in the things that the organization has signaled are worth investing in. Make sure you are sending the right signal about this one.

The Three Conversations Every Leader Needs to Have with Their Team

Beyond the signals you send through behavior, there are three explicit conversations that accelerate the transition to an AI-ready culture. These are not speeches. They are conversations, which means they include listening.

The Permission Conversation

Explicitly tell your team that AI experimentation is expected, not optional, not tolerated, expected. Tell them specifically what kinds of experimentation are in scope, which is most things, and what the guardrails are, which usually come down to data security and disclosure. Remove the ambiguity that has been causing people to hedge.

Most people are not experimenting because they are not sure they are supposed to. This is not stubbornness or lack of interest. It is rational behavior in an environment that has not been explicit about its expectations. Be explicit.

The Anxiety Conversation

Some people on your team are worried about AI. Not because they are technophobes or change-resistant, but because they are paying attention and they have read the same articles you have about what AI is going to do to various categories of work. Some of that concern is well-founded. Most of it is misdirected.

The conversation to have is honest: yes, AI is going to change what some roles look like. No, that is not something that happens to people who develop fluency with AI, because those people become more valuable, not less. The people at risk are the ones who wait for someone else to figure it out and then position themselves as the person who needs to be brought up to speed.

Do not dodge this conversation. Dodging it leaves people with their anxiety and no constructive direction for it. Having it gives them a path.

The Sharing Conversation

Create a standing norm that when someone figures out something useful with AI, they share it with the team. Not in a formal presentation. In a ten-minute conversation at the beginning of a meeting. Here is what I tried. Here is what happened. Here is what I would do differently.

This norm, maintained consistently, compounds in ways that are hard to overstate. At the end of a year, your team has accumulated dozens of shared learnings that individually would have stayed siloed in individual workflows. The team's collective AI fluency is substantially higher than any individual member could have achieved alone. That is a competitive advantage that does not appear on any balance sheet and is very hard for competitors to replicate quickly.

Psychological Safety and AI: The Specific Flavor That Matters Here

There is a specific kind of psychological safety that AI adoption requires and that is slightly different from the general concept.

The general concept is about people feeling safe to speak up, share concerns, and challenge authority. That matters. What AI adoption specifically requires is people feeling safe to be visibly incompetent at something new in front of their colleagues and managers. These are related but not identical.

Learning a new capability involves being bad at it for a while. Most adults find this uncomfortable in professional settings. They are used to being competent. They are used to being the person who knows things. Being the person who is fumbling through a new tool in front of colleagues who might also be fumbling, or worse, might be watching and judging, is a specific kind of vulnerability that shuts down learning fast.

The leader's job here is to model the fumbling. Use AI in a meeting and have it produce something that is not quite right. Make the adjustment out loud. Say: that is not exactly what I wanted, let me try again. Show your team that being in the process of learning this is something a competent, confident person can do publicly without it being a problem.

That one act of visible fumbling does more for your team's willingness to experiment than any number of announcements about the importance of innovation.

CHAPTER 13

The Ethics Layer (The Chapter Everyone Skips and Then Regrets)

I debated whether to include a chapter on AI ethics. Not because I think ethics are unimportant. Because I have noticed that AI ethics chapters in business books tend to be written in a way that manages to be simultaneously preachy and vague, which is a difficult combination to achieve and an unpleasant one to read.

What I want to do instead is give you the specific, practical, executive-level ethical considerations that actually matter in a business context, without the philosophical throat-clearing or the hand-wringing about scenarios that are not going to affect your quarterly objectives.

There are three things in the AI ethics space that executives are genuinely responsible for and that have real consequences if they get wrong. Everything else is mostly interesting to academics and occasionally useful for regulatory compliance.

The First Thing: You Are Responsible for the Outputs, Not the Process

When AI produces something that goes out under your name or your organization's name, you are responsible for it. Not the AI. Not the vendor whose model you used. You. This is not a legal opinion. It is a leadership principle.

This sounds obvious, but its implications are not always followed through. When your team uses AI to produce analysis that informs a major decision, and that analysis turns out to be wrong in a way that has consequences, the defense of the AI was confident about it is not a defense. The AI does not have a reputation to protect. You do.

The practical implication is that every significant AI-assisted output that goes anywhere consequential needs a human review step that is genuinely critical, not performative. Someone who is actually asking: is this right? Is this complete? Is there something missing? Not someone who is reading it quickly on the way to a meeting and nodding.

This is not an argument against using AI. It is an argument for not treating AI outputs as finished products. They are very good first drafts. They need editorial judgment applied to them before they become decisions or communications or strategies.

> *The AI was confident about it is not an explanation your board will find satisfying. Apply your judgment to every significant output. That is what the title is for.*

The Second Thing: Bias Is Invisible Until It Is Very Visible

AI systems can encode and amplify biases in ways that are not obvious until they produce an outcome that is very hard to explain in a public forum. This is not theoretical. It has happened in hiring, in lending, in healthcare triage, in recidivism prediction, in a variety of high-stakes contexts where the people deploying the AI assumed the data would be neutral and discovered that data reflects the world that produced it, which is to say a world that has not been neutral.

For executives, the relevant question is not the philosophical one about whether AI is biased. It is the practical one: in the specific applications where you are deploying or relying on AI in ways that affect people, what are the mechanisms for identifying and correcting problematic patterns?

You do not need to be an AI researcher to answer this question. You need to ask it. Of your technical team. Of your vendors. Of the people building the systems. Ask what bias testing has been done. Ask what happens when a problem is identified. Ask who is responsible for monitoring it over time. The fact of asking sends a signal about what you consider important. The answers tell you whether the people building the systems have thought about it seriously.

The Third Thing: Transparency Is a Competitive Advantage, Not a Compliance Burden

There is a temptation to treat AI disclosure as a legal minimum to be achieved as efficiently as possible. Tell people the minimum required, frame it in language that is technically accurate and practically unintelligible, and move on.

I want to argue for the opposite approach, not primarily on ethical grounds, though those apply, but on strategic ones. Organizations that are genuinely transparent about how they use AI, what it does and does not do, where human judgment applies and where it does not, build a kind of trust that is increasingly scarce and therefore increasingly valuable.

Most organizations are opaque about their AI use by default, either because they have not thought about it carefully or because they are worried about what transparency might reveal. The organizations that choose transparency deliberately stand out. Their customers know what they are getting. Their employees know what the tools are doing. Their stakeholders can make informed assessments.

In an environment where AI-generated content and AI-assisted decisions are becoming ubiquitous and trust is being eroded accordingly, being the organization that is honest about the role AI plays in your work is a differentiating position. It is also, simply, the right thing to do, but I promised not to be preachy, so let us agree that it is both ethical and strategically sensible and leave it there.

Building a Simple AI Ethics Framework Your Organization Can Actually Use

Most AI ethics frameworks that organizations adopt are too complex to use in practice and too abstract to apply to specific situations. The people who would most benefit from them, the ones actually making day-to-day decisions about how to use AI, find them impossible to operationalize and quietly ignore them.

Here is a simpler version. Three questions. Apply them to any significant AI application before you deploy it:

One: If the worst-case output of this system showed up on the front page of a news story about AI gone wrong, would we be comfortable with our role in it? This is not asking whether bad outputs are possible. They always are. It is asking whether you have thought seriously about what they look like and taken reasonable steps to prevent them.

Two: Are the people affected by this system aware that AI is involved, and do they have a meaningful way to seek human review? Meaningful is the key word. A process that technically exists but practically requires a three-week wait and a notarized letter is not meaningful.

Three: Who is responsible for monitoring this application over time, and what are they watching for? AI systems are not static. They change as the models update, as the data they operate on shifts, and as the use cases evolve. Someone needs to own the ongoing responsibility of making sure it is still behaving the way you intended.

These three questions do not cover everything. They cover the things most likely to cause the kinds of problems that are most visible and most costly. Start there.

CHAPTER 14

Measuring AI ROI (The Numbers Your Board Will Actually Ask About)

At some point, someone is going to ask you to justify the investment in AI. Not in a philosophical sense. In a spreadsheet sense. What did we spend, what did we get, how do we know, and when do we get more of it?

This is a reasonable question and also a somewhat tricky one, because many of the most significant returns from AI adoption are not easily captured in the formats that boards and finance committees are accustomed to reviewing. This chapter is about how to measure what can be measured, make a credible case for what cannot, and avoid the two most common mistakes executives make when trying to demonstrate AI ROI.

The Two Most Common Mistakes, So You Can Skip to the Good Part

The first mistake is measuring the wrong things. Most organizations, when they try to measure AI ROI, count things that are easy to count: number of AI tools deployed, percentage of employees who completed AI training, number of prompts submitted per week. These are activity metrics, not outcome metrics. They measure whether AI is being used. They do not measure whether using it is making anything better.

Your board does not care how many prompts your team submitted last quarter. Your board cares whether decisions got better, whether products got better, whether customers are more satisfied, and whether the business is growing. Connect your AI measurement to those things or do not expect it to be taken seriously.

The second mistake is trying to isolate AI as a single variable in a complex system. Revenue went up twenty percent this year. How much of that was the AI? This is an essentially unanswerable question, and attempting to answer it will lead you into a methodological swamp that consumes time and produces numbers nobody trusts. Do not try to isolate. Instead, measure the specific processes where AI was applied and track whether those processes got better.

What to Actually Measure

Time to First Draft

If you are using AI for communication, analysis, or content creation, track how long the process took before AI and how long it takes after. This is a concrete, measurable, defensible number that translates directly into labor cost and capacity. If your team used to spend twelve hours producing a competitive analysis and now does it in three, that is nine hours per analysis times however many analyses you run per year. Put a number on it. Finance people love a number.

Decision Quality Over Time

This is harder to measure but more important. For the specific decisions where you have been using the 4A Pre-Mortem or other AI-assisted decision frameworks, track the outcomes. Are decisions holding up better under scrutiny? Are fewer significant decisions being reversed or significantly modified after implementation? Are the assumptions you documented turning out to be more accurate than they used to be?

You will not get a clean correlation here. The world is complicated. But a qualitative case, supported by specific examples of decisions that were improved by the process, is both honest and persuasive.

Employee Capability Development

Track AI fluency as a capability metric, the same way you track other skills development. Survey your team periodically on their confidence and proficiency. Track how many people have developed specific AI applications in their work. Note the roles where AI fluency has visibly changed the output or the pace of the work.

This is not a substitute for business outcome metrics. It is an input metric that helps you explain the leading indicators before the lagging ones show up in the financials.

The Metrics That Look Good in Reports But Are Not Actually Useful

For completeness, here are the AI metrics that organizations commonly report and that you should treat with appropriate skepticism when you see them.

Cost savings from AI replacing work that would have been done by humans. These numbers are almost always either speculative, because the work was not actually being done before and so there was nothing to replace, or misleading, because the work is still being done but faster, which is productivity, not headcount reduction.

Percentage of employees who have quote-unquote adopted AI. Adoption without impact is noise. Someone who opened an AI tool once in the past month is not an adopter in any meaningful sense. What you want to know is how many people are using AI in ways that are visibly changing their output. That is a smaller number and a more honest one.

Number of use cases identified or pilots launched. Pilots that do not progress to production are a hobby, not a strategy. Count the things that are in production and working, not the things that are being explored.

The Honest Conversation with Your Board

The honest framing for AI ROI conversations with a board is something like this: the returns from AI investment fall into three categories. There are operational returns that are measurable now: time savings, cost reductions in specific processes, quality improvements in specific outputs. There are competitive returns that will materialize over one to three years: better decisions, faster innovation cycles, stronger talent attraction and retention. And there is an optionality value that is harder to quantify: the organizational capability to move quickly as AI continues to evolve, which is worth a great deal in a market where the technology is advancing rapidly and the ability to adapt is a genuine differentiator.

Boards that understand business strategy can engage with this framing. It requires you to be honest about what you know and what you do not, which is considerably more credible than a deck full of numbers that purport to prove what they cannot actually prove.

The leaders who build the most durable AI advantages in their organizations are not the ones who sold their boards on the biggest projected ROI. They are the ones who built genuine capability systematically, measured what mattered, and showed the board the real results over time. That is a slower story to tell and a much better one to be in.

Part Five: The Authority Play

> *How AI-fluent leaders build lasting influence and the career that comes with it*

CHAPTER 15

Thought Leadership in the Intelligence Era (Yes, You Have to Write the Thing)

There is a version of this chapter where I make the case for thought leadership by talking about its strategic importance, its role in building credibility, and its long-term career benefits. I could do that. The argument is solid. Most of you already know it and have filed it under things I agree with and have not done.

So instead let me ask a more interesting question: why haven't you done it?

Not rhetorically. Actually. You have expertise. You have a perspective. You have things to say that would be genuinely useful to the people in your industry. You know this. You have probably been meaning to do something about it for a while. And yet here you are, not having done it.

In my experience working with executives on this specific problem, the answer is almost never lack of ideas. It is almost always some combination of three things: not enough time, not enough confidence that what you have to say is worth saying, and a vague but persistent sense that you will do it properly eventually, when conditions are better.

Let me address all three, in order of how much they are lying to you.

The Time Problem Is Real, and AI Just Solved Most of It

The time problem is legitimate. Producing a well-written, substantive article from scratch takes somewhere between eight and fifteen hours when done well. A book chapter takes longer. A speech takes longer still. For executives running actual organizations, that time does not exist in a form that is reliably available. Something always needs the time more urgently.

AI reduces the time investment for a high-quality article from eight to fifteen hours to two to three hours. For a book chapter, from two to three days to four to six hours. The mechanics of this have been covered in the communication chapter. The point here is strategic: the time argument is no longer what it was. It has been deflated by about seventy percent. If it was the main thing standing between you and a consistent publishing practice, the obstacle is substantially smaller than it used to be.

What remains is the other two problems, which are mostly the same problem wearing different hats.

The Confidence Problem Is Mostly Impostor Syndrome Wearing a Business Suit

The thought leadership confidence problem has a specific shape that I recognize across almost every experienced executive I have worked with on this. It goes like this: everyone in my field already knows the things I would say. The really smart people have said it better. Who am I to add to this conversation?

This is impostor syndrome with a collegial veneer, and it is wrong in a specific and identifiable way.

The people in your field do not all know the things you know. They know the canonical things. The textbook things. The conference circuit things. What they do not know, what they cannot know, is what you have learned by actually doing the work in your specific context with your specific team making your specific mistakes. That knowledge is not in any article or book. It is in you. And the only way it enters the broader conversation is if you put it there.

The executives who publish consistently are not universally the most technically expert people in their fields. They are the ones who got over the question of whether they deserve to be in the conversation and started contributing to it. The contribution itself is what builds the authority. The authority does not have to exist before the contribution. That is not how it works.

> *Nobody waits until they feel ready to start. They start, and then they feel ready. This has been true of every worthwhile thing anyone has ever done, and it is specifically true of thought leadership.*

The Eventually Problem Is the Most Dangerous One

The eventually problem is the most dangerous of the three because it is not experienced as a problem. It is experienced as a reasonable intention. I will write that article eventually. I will start publishing consistently when things quiet down. I will develop my thought leadership platform in the next phase of my career.

Things will not quiet down. The next phase begins when you start, not when circumstances permit. And eventually is a word that has ended more promising trajectories than almost anything else I can name.

Here is the concrete reality: the executive who starts publishing consistently today and the one who starts in two years will be in dramatically different positions in three years. Not because one is smarter or more insightful. Because one has two extra years of compound interest on a visible body of work. Every article generates conversations, introductions, and opportunities that would not otherwise exist. Those compound. The body of work builds on itself. The reputation that forms around it takes on a life of its own.

You cannot go back and start two years ago. You can start today, which is the next best option available and considerably better than starting at some unspecified later date when conditions are right.

AI and Thought Leadership: The Ethics of It, Addressed Briefly

Because this comes up every time: using AI to accelerate your thought leadership is not cheating, provided the ideas are genuinely yours and you would stand behind every word in a live conversation. The assistance is in the execution. The substance is still entirely yours.

The test is simple. Read the finished piece. Ask yourself: do I believe this? Would I say this out loud in a room? Would I defend it under questioning? If the answer to all three is yes, publish it. If any answer is no, revise until it is.

What you are not doing is outsourcing your thinking to AI and attaching your name to its opinions. If you find yourself routinely publishing AI-generated perspectives that you would not have arrived at on your own and that you are not sure you actually agree with, you have crossed a line that is worth stepping back from. Not because anyone will necessarily find out. Because you will know, and it will show eventually in ways that are hard to explain and harder to recover from.

CHAPTER 16

Positioning Yourself as the AI Leader in Your Field (Without Annoying Everyone at Parties)

There is a type of person who became extremely interested in AI approximately eighteen months ago and has since made it their entire personality. They bring it up at dinner. They post about it daily. They have developed the ability to pivot any conversation, regardless of starting topic, to what they are currently building with AI. They are exhausting to be around and have a newsletter that is somehow both too long and not interesting enough.

I want to be very explicit that this is not what I mean by positioning yourself as the AI leader in your field.

What I mean is something considerably more targeted, more durable, and more useful: becoming the person in your specific professional context whose perspective on AI in your industry is worth listening to. Not the person who talks about AI the most. The person whose thinking about AI actually helps people in your field do their jobs better.

That is a specific niche. It is a niche worth owning. And in most industries, it is not yet occupied, which means the opportunity to claim it is available right now to anyone willing to do the work.

Niche Down Until It Gets Uncomfortable, Then Niche Down Again

The most common positioning mistake executives make when building thought leadership is staying too broad. AI thought leadership. Leadership in the digital age. The future of work. These are categories, not positions. They are populated by thousands of people saying similar things at similar levels of generality, and the marginal addition of your voice does not change the landscape in any meaningful way.

The position worth owning is specific: AI for executives in your industry. Or AI and the specific function you spent your career in. Or the intersection of AI and the specific problem your organization exists to solve. The narrower the niche, the less competition, the more relevant you are to the specific people whose attention you want, and the faster you can become genuinely known within it.

I know the instinct is to stay broad so you can reach more people. This instinct is wrong in a very consistent way. Being mildly interesting to a large, diffuse audience produces almost no career benefit. Being genuinely essential to a small, specific audience produces connections, opportunities, speaking invitations, advisory relationships, and the kind of reputation that generates things you did not have to go look for.

Narrow until it is uncomfortable. That discomfort is usually the feeling of a position that is actually distinct enough to be worth holding.

The Platform Stack: What You Actually Need and What You Do Not

There is a version of building a thought leadership platform that involves a podcast, a newsletter, a YouTube channel, a LinkedIn presence, a speaking circuit, a book, and a course, all running simultaneously and all being maintained at a high standard. This version requires either a full-time content team or a clinical inability to sleep.

Most executives do not need that. What you need is a much smaller set of things, maintained consistently, producing quality output over time. Here is the minimal viable platform for an executive who has a day job and wants to build genuine authority in their field:

One Primary Channel, Done Well

Pick the channel where the people you want to reach actually spend their time. For most executives in most industries, this is LinkedIn. For some, it is a newsletter. For some, it is a specific industry publication or conference circuit. Pick one. Do it consistently. Do it at a quality that represents your actual thinking rather than your content calendar.

The executives who build the most durable platforms are not the ones who are everywhere. They are the ones who are reliably excellent in one place. Being reliably excellent in one place is much more achievable and produces better results than being inconsistently present in five places.

A Body of Work That Accumulates

The goal is a body of work that is findable, searchable, and grows over time. An article published eighteen months ago that is still being read and shared is worth more than ten pieces of content that were consumed and forgotten in forty-eight hours. Invest in depth over volume. Produce things that have a longer half-life than the current news cycle. Your analysis of an enduring challenge in your industry, your framework for a problem that executives in your field regularly face, your hard-won perspective on something that the standard advice gets wrong. These things continue working for you long after you have moved on to the next thing.

The Book, Specifically

A book is still the single highest-leverage positioning asset available to a professional. Not because people read books more than they read articles, though many do. Because having written a book signals something about your commitment to a topic that no other medium signals in quite the same way. It says: I thought about this long enough and deeply enough to organize it into something substantial. That signal persists. It shows up in your bio, in introductions at conferences, in the way journalists and podcast hosts and potential clients think about you.

I will not be subtle about what I am doing here. You are holding that book right now. Or you will be, once we finish writing it.

Speaking, Teaching, and the Compound Effect of Showing Up Live

There is something that happens when you present ideas live, in front of an audience, that does not happen when you publish them. You get immediate feedback on what lands and what does not. You develop the ability to explain your ideas in response to real questions rather than imagined ones. You build relationships with the people in the room that a published article cannot build. And you discover, usually faster than you expect, that the nervousness of live presentation fades with repetition and is replaced by something considerably more useful, which is the confidence of someone who has done the thing enough times to know they can do it.

For executives building AI authority specifically, the speaking circuit in most industries is remarkably accessible right now. The demand for credible, experience-based perspectives on AI for leaders is high. The supply of people who have genuinely built things, used the tools in real work, and developed frameworks worth sharing is lower than you might expect. If you have done the work this book describes, you have a talk. Possibly several.

The training program, the advising relationship, the curriculum you build with a partner to bring to organizations: those are the downstream products of the platform. Build the platform first. The rest follows.

CHAPTER 17

Your 90-Day AI Leadership Plan (The Part Where You Actually Do Something)

Every book about doing things differently ends with a plan. This is because the distance between reading about a thing and doing the thing is enormous, and a concrete near-term roadmap is one of the few bridges that reliably spans it. So here is yours.

I have organized it around the LEAD framework, which is the throughline of this book and which I want to make explicit here so you have a single organizing idea to return to when everything gets complicated, which it will.

LEAD — **Leverage** AI for thinking, not just doing. | **Evaluate** every significant output with your judgment. | **Amplify** your unique perspective through consistent output. | **Decide** — the final call is always yours, always.

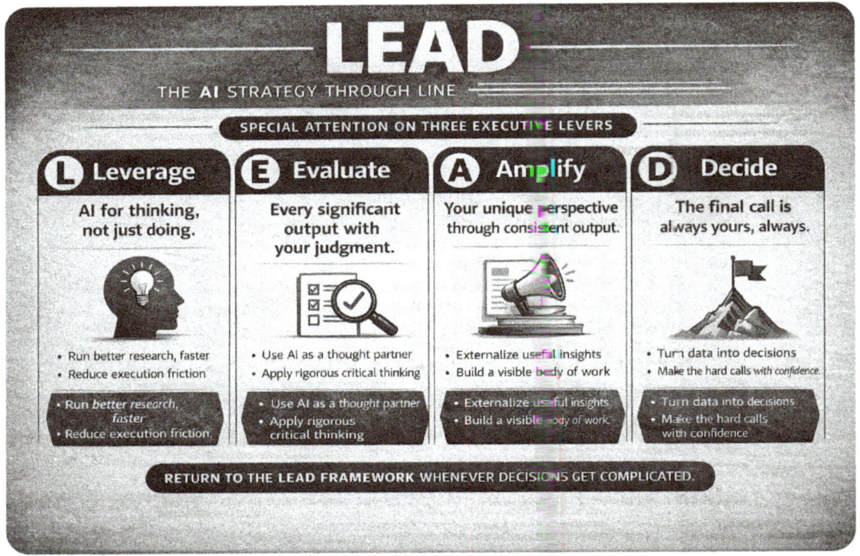

Everything in this ninety-day plan is an expression of one of these four moves. The first thirty days are about Leverage and Evaluate: building your personal practice and developing the critical instincts that make it reliable. Days thirty to sixty are about Amplify: starting to externalize your thinking in ways that build a visible body of work. Days sixty to ninety are about Decide: applying AI-assisted decision intelligence to the real, high-stakes decisions in your work and beginning to bring your team along.

Days 1 to 30: Build Your Practice

Week One: Start With the 4A Pre-Mortem on Something Real

Pick a decision you are currently facing. Not a trivial one. One that has been sitting in the back of your head at eleven o'clock at night. Run the full 4A Pre-Mortem on it. Give it an hour. Be honest about what surfaces.

This is not primarily about improving the decision, though it will probably do that. It is about having your first experience of AI as a genuine thought partner rather than a search engine. That experience will reframe how you think about every subsequent use.

Week Two: Develop Your BRIEF Habit

For every significant AI conversation this week, write out your BRIEF before you start. Background, Role, Intent, Examples, Format. It will feel slow. Do it anyway. By the end of the week it will feel faster. By the end of the month you will be doing it automatically and the quality of your AI interactions will have improved measurably.

Week Three: Run a Competitive Intelligence Exercise

Pick a competitor, a market dynamic, or an industry development that is relevant to your current strategic situation. Spend ninety minutes doing a thorough AI-assisted analysis of it. Apply the So What Chain. See where it takes you.

The goal is not a finished strategic document. The goal is the experience of using AI to think through something that matters, and the calibration of what kind of outputs you can trust and where you need to apply more scrutiny.

Week Four: Have the Three Conversations

Have the Permission Conversation with your team. Have the Anxiety Conversation with the people who need it. Create the first instance of the Sharing Conversation by asking someone who you suspect has been experimenting quietly to share what they have been doing.

These conversations change the environment in ways that all the personal practice in the world cannot substitute for.

Days 30 to 60: Start Amplifying

The First Piece of Content

Write and publish one substantive piece of thought leadership this month. Not a lengthy essay that requires perfect conditions to produce. A clear, specific, experience-based perspective on something that matters in your field. Eight hundred words. One idea developed well.

Use the AI-assisted writing process. Talk through what you want to say. Let AI shape it into a draft. Revise until it sounds like you. Publish it.

The first one is the hardest. It is not perfect. Publish it anyway. The perfect piece of thought leadership that exists only in your head is worth exactly nothing. The imperfect one that exists in the world is worth considerably more.

Identify Your Niche

During this month, spend some time getting specific about the intersection you want to own. Not AI in general. AI in your industry, your function, your specific type of organization. Write it down in a sentence. If it is not specific enough to feel slightly uncomfortable, make it more specific.

Have One AI Conversation a Day

This is the simplest possible habit and also one of the most effective. Once a day, bring a real problem, question, or decision to AI and work through it. Not a trivial question. Something that actually matters. Over thirty days, this produces a compounding effect in your fluency that nothing else quite replicates.

Days 60 to 90: Bring Your Team Along

The First Team Sharing Session

Create a structured opportunity for your team to share AI experiments. A thirty-minute slot at the beginning of an existing meeting. Ask two or three people in advance to share something they tried, what happened, and what they learned. Make it low-stakes, informal, and clear that this is now a thing you do.

Apply AI to a Real Strategic Decision

By this point, you have enough personal practice to bring AI into something that matters at the organizational level. A strategic planning discussion. A competitive response. A major resource allocation decision. Use the tools in this book. Document what you did differently and what you got from it.

Teach One Thing to One Person

Pick someone on your team who would benefit from developing a specific AI skill. Teach them one thing. Specifically: the BRIEF framework, the 4A Pre-Mortem, the So What Chain, or the AI-assisted drafting process. Walk through it with them on a real piece of their work.

Teaching compounds your own understanding. It also begins to distribute the fluency across your team rather than keeping it concentrated in you, which is both more durable and more useful.

The Three Commitments Worth Making Right Now

Before you close this book, I want to ask you to make three commitments. Not to me. To yourself, about this specific ninety-day window.

First: you will open an AI conversation today on something real. Not a test. Not a toy question. A real problem you are actually facing. Start there. Do not wait until you have read more or prepared more or figured out exactly the right first step. The right first step is whatever step you take today.

Second: you will share what you are doing with at least one person on your team this week. Not necessarily everything in this book. One thing. I tried this. Here is what happened. That conversation starts the cultural shift that no individual practice can produce alone.

Third: you will publish one piece of thought leadership in the next thirty days. It does not have to be long. It does not have to be perfect. It has to exist, and it has to represent your actual thinking. That is enough to start.

The executives who make these three commitments and keep them will, in ninety days, be materially different from where they are today. Not transformed. Not unrecognizable. But specifically, measurably more capable, more visible, and more positioned for what is coming next.

The ones who do not make them will read a very good book and then continue exactly as before.

I have told you everything I know. The rest is yours.

CHAPTER 18

Conclusion: The Leader Who Thinks with AI

I want to come back to the octopus.

Not literally. We have established that I have the standard number of arms. But the idea of the octopus as a metaphor for what becomes possible when your capacity to execute matches your capacity to think, that idea is the one I want to leave you with.

For most of my career, the bottleneck was execution. I knew what I wanted to make. I could see it. I understood how it should look, feel, and function. The constraint was always the gap between the thing in my head and the thing I could actually produce with the resources and time available. That gap produced compromises. Projects I did not start. Ideas I let go. Good work that was not as good as it could have been because the execution had limits the vision did not.

AI closed that gap for me in ways I did not fully anticipate when I started using it. Not by replacing my thinking. By giving my thinking a surface to work against that was fast enough and capable enough that the constraint shifted from execution to vision. The question stopped being what can I actually make and became what do I actually want to make. That is a different and considerably more interesting question.

I think the same shift is available to leaders. The executives who develop genuine AI fluency, who learn to think with AI rather than just through AI, will find that the constraint shifts from execution to vision in their professional lives as well. The question stops being what can I actually accomplish given the resources and time I have and becomes what do I actually want to build. What does the organization I actually want to lead look like. What is the contribution I actually want to make.

That is not a small change. That is the whole game.

> *The leaders who will define the next decade are not the ones who adopted AI the fastest. They are the ones who let it change what they believed was possible.*

Everything in this book is in service of that shift. The RAT Trap, the 4A Pre-Mortem, the AMP framework, the BRIEF, the LEAD. These are not tricks. They are the scaffolding for a different relationship with your own capability.

You do not need to implement all of it at once. You do not need to become an AI expert. You need to start, and then keep going, and pay attention to what changes as you do. The compound returns show up slowly and then all at once, and by the time they show up all at once, the investment will have felt completely worth it.

I have one more thing to tell you, and I want to say it plainly.

The executives who told me they were too busy, too senior, too set in their approach to learn this new thing, who thought their existing capability was sufficient, who planned to revisit the question when things settled down, those executives are further behind today than they were when we had that conversation. Not catastrophically. Just measurably. And the gap is growing, quietly, in the way all important gaps grow.

You read this book. That means you decided it was worth your time. That decision was correct. Now make the next one.

The AI Implementation Lab is open. Come find me there.

CHAPTER 19

Appendix A: The Executive AI Audit

Before you can measure progress, you need a baseline. This brief self-assessment is designed to give you an honest picture of where you and your organization are today. There are no right answers and no scores. There is only an honest account of your starting position, which is more useful than a flattering one.

Personal Fluency

1. How often do you use AI in your actual work, not counting search? Daily, weekly, occasionally, or rarely?
2. When you use AI, do you iterate through multiple rounds to refine the output, or do you typically use the first response?
3. Have you used AI to pressure-test a significant decision in the past three months?
4. Have you used AI to produce communication that went to an external audience?
5. Could you explain, concretely, how AI has changed something about how you work?

Organizational Readiness

1. Do your team members have explicit permission to use AI in their work, or is the policy ambiguous?
2. Does your organization have any forum, however informal, for sharing AI learnings across teams?

3. Can you name three people on your team who are more AI-fluent than average and what they are doing with it?
4. Has AI come up in any significant strategic conversation in your organization in the past six months?
5. Does your organization have a clear position on AI transparency with customers and stakeholders?

What to Do With Your Answers

The areas where you hesitated or answered no are your starting points. Not everything needs to be addressed at once. Pick the two that would have the highest impact if improved and make them the focus of the first thirty days of your plan.

CHAPTER 20

Appendix B: The Five Frameworks at a Glance

The RAT Trap

RAT TRAP — **Resisters** wait for AI to prove itself. **Adopters** collect tools without developing fluency. **Thinkers** change how they think. Most leaders are stuck in the Resister or Adopter position. The goal of this book is to help you escape the trap and become a Thinker.

BRIEF

BRIEF — **Background**: What's the situation? | **Role**: Who should AI be in this conversation? | **Intent**: What are you trying to accomplish? | **Examples**: What does a good output look like? | **Format**: How should the response be structured?

The 4A Pre-Mortem

4A PRE-MORTEM — **Assumptions**: What am I taking for granted that might be wrong? | **Absent Information**: What am I not accounting for? | **Adversarial Case**: What is the strongest argument against my position? | **Arm's-Length View**: What would I tell someone else to do if this were their decision?

AMP

AMP — **Analysis**: Compress research cycles and stress-test strategy faster than ever before. | **Messaging**: Eliminate the blank page and develop your executive voice at scale. | **Positioning**: Build the thought leadership body of work that compounds over time.

LEAD

LEAD — **Leverage** AI for thinking, not just doing. | **Evaluate** every significant output with your judgment. | **Amplify** your unique perspective through consistent output. | **Decide** — the final call is always yours.

About the Author

Before he was writing books about publishing, Robert Moutal was making television. His career in broadcast media, including 16-time Emmy Award-winning work at Telemundo and Univision San Diego, gave him a front-row seat to how stories get made, packaged, and sold to audiences at scale.

These days, he applies that same lens to the world of indie authors. As a self-publishing coach, he's worked with hundreds of writers on everything from cover strategy to market positioning. He's also the founder of Cover Design App and Translato.ai, AI-powered tools that help independent authors compete smarter. And as co-founder of AI Implementation Lab, he helps everyday entrepreneurs move past AI curiosity into actual, practical use.

When he's not building things or teaching, Robert is based in San Diego, where he lives with his wife and their dog, and occasionally his three adult kids, depending on who needs what.

www.ingramcontent.com/pod-product-compliance
Lightning Source LLC
LaVergne TN
LVHW010934110826
845149LV00013B/2590

* 9 7 8 1 9 6 8 6 3 9 0 9 9 *